ISBN 978-0-578-80157-5

Library of Congress Control Number: 2020922352
Library of Congress subject headings:
College student orientation
College student orientation United States
College students
College students Conduct of life
College students Life skills guides
Education Student Life & Student Affairs
Handbooks and manuals
High school students
Life skills guides
Reference Personal & Practical Guides

Cover designed by David Wu

Printed in the United States of America

Published by B&B Publishing
http://suzybohnert.wix.com/gameday

I0122696

ATTENTION SCHOOLS AND BUSINESSES

B&B Publishing books are available at quantity discounts with bulk purchase for educational, business, or sales promotional use. For information, please e-mail the B&B Publishing Special Sales Department at bandbpublishing@hotmail.com.

College, Covid, and Questions:
Tips and Advice for Incoming Freshmen, Undergraduates, Transfer Students, and Parents

Millions of people are considering going on to college, but there are so many choices and questions that need consideration and answers. Not only when and where do you want to go to school, but once you've made the decision, how do you prepare? Once on campus, how do you take advantage of all the opportunities at college and beyond? What type of school — community college, four-year university, public, or private?

Whether you're in high school, the mom or dad of a university student, taking a gap year or a college transfer student, making a career change, finishing a military career, or enduring a bad job market, this book is for you. Or, maybe you were waiting for your dream school, and received an acceptance.

College, Covid, and Questions will help you to know:

- School essentials during coronavirus
- Considerations when buying a computer
- Technology to succeed in school
- Characteristics to look for in a tutor
- Advice on help with accommodations and services from the Center for Accessibility Services
- Advantages and disadvantages of campus meal plans
- Hints and tips when seeking an internship
- Tips to get along with roommates
- Academic advisors — your role and theirs

Simple, clear answers about coronavirus and college, classes, internships, campus dining, dorms, roommates and residence life, academic advisors and mentors, clubs, recreational activities, and getting back home. This is the essential guide to navigating the college journey successfully in these unprecedented times.

By Suzy Beamer Bohnert
Copyright © 2020
All Rights Reserved

Also by Suzy Beamer Bohnert

Binkie Learns to Fly

Game-Day Goddess: Learning Baseball's Lingo

Game-Day Goddess: Learning Basketball's Lingo

Game-Day Goddess: Learning Football's Lingo

Game-Day Goddess Sports Series, 3-Volume Set

Game-Day Youth: Learning Baseball's Lingo

Game-Day Youth: Learning Basketball's Lingo

Game-Day Youth: Learning Football's Lingo

TABLE OF CONTENTS

DEDICATION

For Rand and Carolyn, who always ask the best questions.

PREFACE

While there are a variety of books to help you get into college, there are very few that help you navigate the college scene once you receive admittance, transfer to a different university, or start attending classes on campus. Even parents have questions to ask about the university experience because things may have changed since their days at college, or maybe they never set foot on a campus and don't know the first thing to ask.

This book came about for this very reason. Bewildered by the number of colleges out there and their differences, we looked for one source to answer a multitude of questions in one place. We found SAT test practice books, college rankings and ratings, and how-to books on writing college essays, but nothing that helped with how to ask and have questions answered when you don't know what you don't know.

Coming up with questions was not hard. We knew nothing and moved on from there to involve university representatives, trade association spokesmen, company and government agency personnel, and students themselves in answering our questions. What resulted was a guidebook for parents of prospective college students, incoming freshmen, college transfer students, and those now studying at universities. The book deals with all aspects of college, and it does answer these important questions.

Coronavirus and College

Now that coronavirus has affected the United States and every college campus, things are different at each school. Institutions have implemented measures to make sure students and school employees stay safe and healthy, and staff on campus do things another way now.

Many colleges have implemented new public-health measures. Here are some things you might expect to see on campus:

Handwashing or hand sanitizer

Doctors have recommended washing your hands often using soap and water — lathering your hands for at least 20 seconds. Hand sanitizer also works well, and you will see dispensers at points throughout campus to help you. "If soap and water are not readily available, hand sanitizer that contains at least 60% alcohol can be used," the Centers for Disease Control and Prevention says.

Mask or face coverings

Many universities are handing out masks for free to all students. When walking to class or in a classroom, wear your face covering. The same holds if you are meeting with a professor or in a common area. When outside, wear a mask and stay six feet from others. Practice social distancing to the maximum extent possible.

Physical distancing

Classrooms, offices, and campus spaces are now set up to have six feet of distance between individuals. Look for markings on floors to see proper spacing. Additionally, many buildings will have one-way corridors clearly marked to enhance social distancing. Be sure to follow directional signs.

Not touching your face

Germs spread from hands to your eyes, nose, and mouth when you touch your face. Expect to see signs and reminders around campus of this important fact.

Don't go out when sick

When feeling ill or after exposure to someone with a positive test for Covid-19, stay in your location and keep track of your symptoms. Your health-care facility or the Dean's Office can advise you on making appointments and how to handle the situation.

What to have with you at school

Health-insurance card

A photocopy of this card is important for the health-care facility on campus to assist you or, if you need treatment at a hospital or other facility, this card will provide needed information.

Hand sanitizer

Have some hand sanitizer in your room and backpack. Look for hand-sanitizer dispensers around campus.

Disinfectant cleaner

Use disinfectant cleaner to clean things touched frequently, including the faucet handles, door knobs, light switches, and appliances in your dorm or apartment.

Thermometer

Use this to track your temperature each day. Some schools require you to perform and report results of a daily temperature check.

Face coverings and masks

While the university may supply you with masks, bring extras. Make sure to wash these face coverings frequently to ensure their effectiveness.

Tracking symptoms, testing, and contact tracing

Your university may have you complete a daily tracking survey, which asks questions about your health and any unusual symptoms that you may have. All students attending on-campus classes and events would complete this survey.

The CDC recommends to "conduct daily health checks or ask faculty, staff, and students to conduct the self-checks of temperature screening and/or symptom checking."

According to the CDC, "People with Covid-19 have had a wide range of symptoms reported — ranging from mild symptoms to severe illness. Symptoms may appear **two-14 days after exposure to the virus.** People with these symptoms may have Covid-19:

- Fever or chills
- Cough
- Shortness of breath or difficulty breathing
- Fatigue
- Muscle or body aches
- Headache
- New loss of taste or smell
- Sore throat
- Congestion or runny nose
- Nausea or vomiting
- Diarrhea

This list does not include all possible symptoms."

Testing

Once arriving on campus for the start of the school year, staff would test for the coronavirus and you would receive results via a campus communication system. For students who have Covid-19 symptoms following initial campus testing, the student health center will administer an additional test. For those who test positive after initial testing, staff will contact and test close contacts.

Contact tracing

Universities typically will work with state Departments of Health to conduct contact tracing for those suspected of having close contact with someone who has tested positive for coronavirus.

Classes

At many universities, look for classroom chairs spaced six feet apart. Teachers are at the front of the classroom with plastic partitions in front of them while they lecture, allowing for safe separation from students. These classrooms most likely will have fewer than 50 students, and some larger rooms will host smaller classes.

For those classes with more than 50 students, the university may provide online instruction. Online instruction will also be available to those who may not be on campus or who prefer to take courses virtually rather than being in a classroom.

Generally, classes may be online, smaller, or in-person, and school facilities may have reduced hours due to the need for additional cleaning.

When possible, use flexible work or learning sites (e.g., telework, virtual learning) and flexible work or learning hours (e.g., staggered shifts or classes) to help establish policies and practices for social distancing (maintaining distance of approximately six feet) between people, especially if state and local health authorities recommend social distancing.

The CDC "encourage students, faculty, and staff to use disinfectant wipes to wipe down shared desks, lab equipment, and other shared objects and surfaces before use." Additionally, it says, "Avoid sharing electronic devices, books, pens, and other learning aids."

Tutoring and office hours with professors

As it applies to tutoring and office hours with professors, many schools may heed CDC guidance, which is to "replace in-person meetings with videoconference or teleconference calls whenever possible. Provide student support services virtually, as feasible."

Housing

For the safety of all, when in dorms, students should wear masks when in all public places, including hallways, laundry rooms, lobbies, and lounges.

If you plan to use the kitchen in a dorm, you may have to have a key to use this shared space or there may be signs posted or floor indicators to let you know of social-distancing requirements.

In many instances, schools may not allow guests in dorms or off-campus apartments.

The CDC says, in cases where a roommate "has been sick with Covid-19 symptoms, tested positive for Covid-19, or has been potentially exposed to someone with Covid-19," you and others living in that apartment or dorm room may have been exposed. In this case, if you have been exposed to someone for more than 15 minutes from six feet or less, then you should seek medical guidance and let the campus health-care group know you have been exposed. Medical personnel may ask you to quarantine.

Many colleges have dorms and apartments off-campus available to you for the purpose of quarantining. The CDC recommends "to identify an isolation room, area, or building/floor (for on-campus housing) to separate anyone who has Covid-19 symptoms or tests positive, but does not have symptoms."

To lower the risk of contracting coronavirus, some universities have instituted move-in hours at the start of the semester with shifts and days assigned to students to limit interaction among those living in the same hallway of a dorm or the same floor of an apartment building.

Student life

Student organizations, school events, and recreational spaces may still take place and be open, typically with a limit to the number of participants. Using online programs, such as Zoom, may allow more people to participate in these activities. For off-campus activities, for example those of sororities and fraternities, these events may have group-size limitations enforced by school officials. Violations of social rules may result in expulsion because large, off-campus social gatherings may result in Covid-19 hot spots.

Campus resources, such as the library, gym, student union, and computer labs will likely be open, but with reduced hours for additional cleaning. Gyms may be open for individual activities such as weightlifting, but with fewer or no team sports available. For all activities, they feature social-distancing measures separating students by six feet.

Many schools may hold Parents' Weekend online. Regarding sports, there may be no athletic events at your campus and no fans in the stands at football games, if the games take place. As the CDC says, "Promote social distancing of at least six feet between people if events are held. Limit group size to the extent possible."

Dining halls

Schools may require students to eat in a dining hall only with members of their dorm. Additionally, tables and chairs will separate students by six feet, and you will most likely not have self-service stations or buffets, but instead, packaged food. You may be able to sit at a table with your roommate.

Other eateries, including fast-food outlets, may require you to order a meal in advance and pick it up at the merchant's location to grab-and-go.

Health centers

Many health centers at campuses nationwide will offer telehealth visits, so that you don't need to come into the facility, unless the health-center staff asks you to visit or you would like to make an in-person appointment. A feature of many health centers will be a well area and a sick area to keep patients safe.

Mental health

Many sources have indicated young adults are experiencing greater anxiety since the onset of Covid-19. For that reason, the CDC says, "Encourage employees and students to take breaks from watching, reading, or listening to news stories, including social media, if they are feeling overwhelmed or distressed.

"Promote employees and students eating healthy, exercising, getting sleep, and finding time to unwind."

Campus bus systems

For those taking the bus, many universities are blocking off every other row in buses and limiting one student per row. Some are asking students to board and exit the bus in the rear, to avoid the spread of coronavirus.

"Commute during less busy times and clean hands as soon as possible after their trip," the CDC says. "Encourage students, faculty and staff who use public transportation or ride sharing to use forms of transportation that minimize close contact with others (e.g., biking, walking, driving, or riding by car either alone or with household members)."

Classes

What about tutors? What tutoring is available to me?

What about tutors?

Tutors can help students in many ways in subjects as varied as math, business, humanities, social sciences, and natural sciences. While they don't do the work for you, they teach you skills to complete your school tasks. Importantly, tutoring-services departments have individuals who cover not only academic topics, but helpful things, such as note-taking, managing time, test-taking strategies, and improving study skills.

At many campuses, tutors are not an additional cost to students and benefit those who want to keep or raise their grades. Often, tutors are important in student retention.

Any advice on when you should seek tutoring help?

As to when to seek tutoring, students should ask for help as soon as they are having difficulty understanding the material. Not understanding foundational information will make later learning more difficult and catching up hard to do. Professors know and understand the material and recognize what they want students to learn, so students should first talk to their professors during office hours when they initially encounter difficulty. Depending on the professor's receptiveness and helpfulness, students may find the professor a valuable resource. Many faculty members want students to use office hours. Students will probably need to see tutors in addition to their professor, partly because of limitations on office hours and time with the professor.

If you're having a problem in a specific class, it's better to get a tutor right away rather than reluctantly finding a tutor after your grade plummets to a D or an F. If you're not having a problem in the class, meeting with a tutor is a way to refine your skills regarding a specific topic, or prepare yourself for an upcoming test or project, a Radford University student says.

What tutoring is available to me?

Campus-wide tutoring will be available to all students, but sessions may be all virtual. Underserved students participating in state-funded programs, including the Educational Opportunity Program (EOP) or

COLLEGE, COVID, AND QUESTIONS
COLLEGE, COVID, AND QUESTIONS

federally-funded programs like Student Support Services (SSS) or the intersegmental program (University of California, California Department of Education, California State University, California Community Colleges) Mathematics, Engineering, Science Achievement (MESA), may have tutoring services available to them.

It's not unusual for more tutoring to be available for general-education classes rather than upper-level courses. If you are in a smaller major, there may not be as much of a supply of tutors, says a Radford University student.

Is there much tutoring available for 300- and 400-level classes?

Tutoring for 300- and 400-level classes typically taken by upperclassmen will depend on the tutoring program. Most will focus on 100- and 200-level courses taken by freshmen and sophomores. If tutors are available for 300- and 400-level courses, these classes typically tend to be frequently-requested STEM classes featuring science, technology, engineering, and mathematics topics, and business courses.

What should a student look for in a tutor?

When seeking a tutor, look for certain qualities, says Dr. Howard Masuda, a former director of the University Tutorial Center at California State University, Los Angeles. "Being friendly and welcoming, courteous, receptive and willing to help, caring, encouraging, patient, a good listener, and knowledgeable about the subject and able to communicate this knowledge in response to questions in a clear and concise manner," are all important things for a tutor to possess, he said. Helpful qualities include someone honest about the limits of their knowledge and someone who makes students the center of the session. A tutor who constantly provides opportunities and encourages students to participate in the session by showing what they know, understand, and can do are essential.

The tutors are people with knowledge of the class because they took it previously. Sometimes, only one professor teaches a class, so the tutor might be acquainted with the teacher as well, says a Radford University student.

Look for a tutor who's passionate about the topic and respectful to you. You might not understand the topic well — after all, that's why you're receiving tutoring — and you want the tutor to be caring and understanding and not get frustrated with you as you try to learn the subject, Masuda said.

8

How does the typical tutoring arrangement work on campus?

During a college career, everyone will need help with course content that baffles them. Make it a point to learn more about how the typical tutoring arrangement works on campus.

Students can usually find tutors in a learning assistance or tutoring center on campus. Some academic departments may also provide tutoring. Learners normally self-refer to either of these groups, and depending on the program, tutoring can be provided on a different basis, including a one-to-one scheduled appointment, reserved group tutoring, unplanned walk-in tutoring, or organized online tutoring.

On some campuses, student tutors must not only have passed the class they tutor, but have earned a grade of B or better. Look on your school's Web site to see if there is a tutoring site that features the student name of individual tutors, the classes they teach, and the times the tutor is available. To sign up, you may go into the university portal and indicate which class you need help for and what times you are available. The schedule might list the available tutors for the times you are free. Then, you go to the tutoring session, which may be in the library or perhaps another academic building on campus. You may sign up for as many sessions during the week as you would like, says a Radford University student, and he typically signs up for the same tutor.

What things should a student do to prepare for a tutoring session?

To prepare for a tutoring session, students must attempt to read the textbook assignment and try to answer the questions or problems. Identify what is not clear in the textbook and class notes to make the best use of time with a tutor because lecturing about an entire topic is not one of the roles of a tutor.

Because there is typically a time limit on the tutoring, don't waste time being unprepared. Try to do some of the problems or writing before you meet with the tutor, and don't expect the tutor to teach you everything during one tutoring session. Use your notes from class and prepare specific questions for the tutor to make the most of your time, a Radford University student says.

Identify specific concepts and problems going into the session for which you need assistance. With limited time, cover what is most important to you first.

How often and how long should a typical tutoring session last?

According to Masuda, content area tutoring sessions typically last an hour; writing tutoring sessions usually last 30 minutes. Programs may limit the number of tutoring appointments per week, which students may schedule. Walk-in or drop-in, if offered, tend to be of unlimited time, although students may have to wait until tutors take each student in turn.

What happens if a tutor doesn't work out? What should a student do?

If a tutor doesn't work, there are options. At the beginning, a student may want to try working with different tutors, assuming they have a choice. This can be helpful in a situation where their regular tutor is absent, and they need to find another tutor. Having worked with other tutors, a student can more easily select one who meets their needs.

Wanting to do the best they can, tutors may ask the pupil for suggestions at the end of a session as to how they could improve the tutoring. Be honest. Even if the tutors don't ask, students can make suggestions to the tutors about what works best for them. Changing a tutor may be awkward, but generally can take place by talking to the scheduling staff or the supervisor. A student needs to do what is best for him.

It's not a requirement to have only one tutor for a class. However, for some subjects that are more uncommon, there may be only one available tutor. Typically, for general education classes there are multiple tutors, so if you don't like the tutor or if the tutor's schedule doesn't mesh with yours, you're not locked in with one tutor, says a Radford University student.

Are there recommendations on how to structure your tutoring session?

"Many tutoring programs base the structure of their tutoring sessions on the twelve steps of the Tutor Cycle by Dr. Ross MacDonald or some variation of the Cycle, which you can find at this Web site: http://www.cambridgestratford.com/tutoring/tutorassessments.html. Knowing this structure can help a student know what to expect and the reasons for the tutors' actions," says Masuda.

If you have a class that meets just once a week, don't wait awhile to set up a tutoring session because you want to have the material fresh in your mind. By getting a tutor quickly, this setup would likely allow you to remember what the teacher said in class about a specific assignment or test, allowing you to profit from the quickness with which you scheduled a tutoring session.

What tips do you have when working with a tutor?

Come prepared and assume you will work with the tutor in an interactive, collaborative manner and expect to participate in the session. Anticipate the textbook and course notes to be the main sources of information. Understand that tutors know and understand a lot about the subject matter, but they are still students and not experts. Don't expect them to know everything. When tutors do not know the answer, presume they will consult with other tutors and offer to work with you using the textbook, class notes, and the Internet to discover the answer.

Tutoring tips

Be ready to do your homework with the help of a tutor, but never expect your tutor to do your work.

Do the reading and writing in advance of your tutoring meeting. For textbook and class notes you don't understand, commit to paper what you need the tutor to help you with and show them the section of the book or notes where you're having problems. From there, do you want the tutor to help with organizing your work, use examples to explain a topic, see if you understand your classwork, or show you the techniques for explaining solutions to problems? Discuss with the tutor what areas you most need help with to make your session successful.

Things to bring to the tutoring session include your laptop or iPad, books, class notes and syllabus, teacher handouts, assignments — whether finished or not — and paper, pencils, erasers, and calculators. Tutors don't bring these materials, but you should.

Arrive for your appointment on time. If you don't, some schools will cancel the tutoring session or offer it to someone else. If you can't make your appointment, call, e-mail, or text to cancel and leave a message on the tutoring session answering machine with your name, appointment time, your tutor's name, and your phone number.

When time allows, check to see if your appointment is on time. Many times, you can consult your calendar and book your next tutoring session before your lesson begins.

Tutors are meant to help you, but not do your work. Ask them to show you and explain things you don't understand. Most tutoring centers don't allow tutors to write or proofread papers, solve an entire problem, or help you with extra credit, quizzes, or exams. You will want to learn how to do what is necessary to take the test or write the paper, so learn from the tutor what information and ideas are necessary for you to understand to do well. Do you need to talk about those things, go over main points, recite, problem-solve, calculate? How do you make connections and show how things relate to other things?

When working with a tutor, if you don't understand something, ask them to explain or go over material again.

Arrive ready to learn, with your materials, prepared to discuss your assignment. It's important that you went to class, took notes, and read the textbook before your tutoring session. Don't jeopardize your chance at future tutoring by not taking it seriously.

For problems with a tutor, try to work with that person. If that doesn't help, ask tutoring-office staff for help to resolve the issue.

Where would you find out more about tutoring?

To learn more about campus tutoring, searching college Web sites will help locate available tutoring services. For instance, at Masuda's previous Cal State University, Los Angeles, campus, click on http://branding.calstatela.edu/tutorialcenter/about-center to find out more about tutoring.

You can also go into the campus tutoring center to inquire about services.

What about the class selection process and access to advisors?

What about the class selection process and access to advisors?

To choose classes, every student will have an academic advisor assigned to them. They might meet in person or virtually. It's important to remember that the student and the advisor have specific duties.

As a student, make the most of the time with an advisor, and do the following things:

- Get on your advisor's schedule early in the semester to begin planning for the next semester.
- Ask the advisor what classes prospective employers are looking for.
- Seek out information from the advisor about the current job market and what to do now to improve job prospects.
- To graduate on time, see what undergraduate classes you need to meet requirements for your major and the university and confirm these with the advisor.
- Come up with a class schedule for the upcoming semester and be aware of semester deadlines.
- Once you decide on a certain schedule, don't change it unless you talk to the advisor first.
- Take advantage of discussing other topics. Subjects might include internships; study abroad; jobs; clubs; changing your major; summer school; and academic challenges and progress.
- Ask to have an academic advisor assigned to you for your entire undergraduate experience, as well as a student mentor in your major who can provide helpful tips.
- Make sure to read and respond, if necessary, to items that come from the advisor, academic college, or the advising center.
- Be on time to meet the advisor or cancel an appointment and reschedule if a conflict arises.

Academic advisors should do the following:

- Set up a scheduling system to meet with you and return your phone calls and e-mails.
- Know and give correct information about deadlines, classes, departments, and the requirements to graduate on time.

- Focus on your area of study and develop with you a manageable class schedule that allows you to thrive after considering your abilities, goals, and personal obligations.
- Keep you on track to meet your career goals and show you how to prepare for your intended objectives.
- For those with special needs, point you to on-campus services and opportunities.
- Monitor your progress toward educational goals and keep accurate, up-to-date records of academic progress.
- Safeguard your educational records and keep confidential information limited to those who need to know.
- Work with you to make appropriate decisions and actions regarding your academic career.

When registering for classes, typically the seniors enroll first, followed by priority groups, such as those signed up with the accessibility services office and sometimes those undergraduates who are active-duty military. Next would be juniors and sophomores, ending with freshmen.

What technology do I need to get through school?

What technology do I need to get through school?

Each school is different. Some require students to bring a laptop to college, while others don't. At other universities, students can bring computers with whatever computer operating system they want; others specify if the university supports Macintosh or Windows.

Smartphones — either an iPhone or an Android phone — are important for students. For instance, Blackboard and Canvas are two educational platforms used by many college professors to post class assignments and materials. Students can access these platforms and their coursework from their phone.

Students are on their smartphones all the time: with their phones, they can access their coursework, they can order ahead from a dining hall. A smartphone is important for students at a college. That's another expensive purchase for college though, and none of this is cheap, and it's an investment for families.

As for other technology, while a laptop and a smartphone are requirements, a printer is optional. You might want to consider an iPad for books because using Kindle to have an online book is often half the price of a regular textbook. You can even rent books through Kindle or other book services and it's so much cheaper.

"As for technology that we don't recommend students have, wireless printers are the big thing. In general, I tell parents not to buy a printer and see how they can do without it. However, in a case where every professor asks that you print class notes, I absolutely understand why a student has a printer in his room. That makes a lot of sense," says Laurie Fox, director of educational technology at SUNY Geneseo.

Final word is to get a good backpack that is comfortable and will protect the laptop.

What are some barriers you might need to address if most learning is virtual?

For students attending classes virtually, keep in mind a bigger computer screen, faster Internet, and noise-canceling headphones may well be worth the investment.

Any type of computer or printer you suggest a student not purchase?

"Although Chromebooks are popular in grades kindergarten through 12th grade, they are not a computer that's appropriate for college because they have little storage space and they are processors with low power," Fox says.

How about Internet access — how does that work on a typical college campus?

Internet access and Wi-Fi are hot issues. Wireless networking is another topic that colleges are really looking at because the students need good Wi-Fi to do pretty much everything. In the residence halls it becomes a blend of doing homework while watching Netflix. Often, the number one network user is Netflix. Technology departments are constantly working to increase the capacity of their Wi-Fi, and that is true on any college campus.

Any tips to maintain access to the best possible Internet when all the students in the dorm or off-campus housing are trying to do the same thing?

When students complain that the wireless is slow, look to see where they are in relationship to the Wi-Fi wireless access point — typically on the wall or ceiling. In high-density areas like the library, the college uses a lot of antennas that have direction capability, so that it can cover a specific area. Wireless network access is a shared pipe, so if you are in a crowded Starbucks, for example, it's going to be slower for you than in a smaller Starbucks with only two people there. For students who are in the library, if they are not getting good Internet, look at who is around you and sit in a less crowded area.

Here's where an up-to-date computer with up-to-date drivers and an operating system will help students, too. If you're working on an older computer that might have an older wireless card, you're not able to take advantage of the newer wireless technology.

How about printers with Wi-Fi capabilities? Should you use those and worry about everyone sending their assignments to your printer?

Printers with Wi-Fi. No, no, no. Most campuses don't allow them on the network.

Can you make do without a printer, or is that essentially a necessity?

Fox says, "My philosophy is that people can make do without a printer, but people are going to have to make decisions for themselves."

COLLEGE, COVID, AND QUESTIONS

What kind of technology support does a university provide?

What kind of technology support does a typical university provide?

Technology support handles many general items for students. For instance, a student may need their account password reset or university software installed. Regarding smartphones, help-desk technicians will help them get their smartphone on the Internet and install campus apps. If there's a problem with a student's printer or computer in their dorm, they can give the staff at the help desk a call or visit the help desk for assistance, says Alex, a freshman staff member at the University of Iowa Hawk help desk.

Students typically come to the walk-in location for service. However, if there's a problem with a printing station on campus or in a university classroom, help-desk teams will go to the location and fix those issues. While some help-desk personnel will not go into dorm rooms to assist, there are other universities that offer a service where they visit student rooms to provide support. Because of coronavirus, some help-desk personnel ask that you bring your computer or printer to the help desk for service. Some colleges offer more services, but many don't. For many, they don't offer any hardware repair and won't help students reinstall their operating system or that sort of thing.

Are there certain apps that students should have on their cell phone? If so, which ones?

Alex suggests that students set up an e-mail account on their phone to access university e-mails. For notices for things such as an active shooter on campus, his university has what's called a Hawk Alert, which is similar to the campus alert system on most campuses. Basically, an alert goes to the e-mail or phone number a student has on file, allowing them to get a text, an e-mail, or a phone call notifying them about what's going on.

For grading, schools typically have an online system that professors use to post assignments and grades as well as slides and lectures. It's accessible with any Web browser and is an icon you'll want to have on your home page to offer easy access to this important information.

Laurie Fox adds that there are certain apps schools may recommend. At many colleges, such as SUNY Geneseo where Fox works as director of educational technology, they have an app named for the college and called the Geneseo app. The school also offers Canvas, an academic platform, and a software called Rave Guardian that is a personal safety application. This safety application works in this manner. Say a student is walking back from the library to his dorm room. He could send a message to a friend saying that he is heading back to his dorm room, and the friend can see that he gets back safely. More colleges are offering that type of application to students.

Additionally, Geneseo has a new product where students can make advising appointments or get help by using their cell phone. Because Geneseo is a Google campus, all students can use Google applications on their phones. Fox says some faculty use a product called Top Hat. While ten years ago a professor might have used a clicker to show slides or a presentation, now they use their phones to perform the same function.

Any recommendations on how to handle technology issues?

Alex says, "To assist someone at the help desk to solve a problem, provide specific details about the issue. If the first person you contacted at the help desk cannot assist you, they will ask a supervisor or direct the issue to a team that specializes in whatever matter needs a solution."

Fox adds, "Students should call the help desk for any technology issues, because even if it's not part of the stated services on campus, usually the person handling the call can direct you to the proper place, so that's helpful in solving any problems."

Are there opportunities to get free software and major-specific programs through universities?

"Many students at campuses automatically have a Microsoft license agreement, which means they can install the Microsoft Office Suite for free on their computer. If the university provides additional licensing agreements, students can also put those software programs on other devices as well," Alex says. This will vary from college to college, so when you look at schools, you need to see what software they offer to students.

"While many colleges may offer Microsoft Office, they might also have major-specific software, such as Minitab, Spartan, Matlab, Mathematica, and some chemistry software. It's a good idea for students to look and see what software is available to them from the school before they buy programs," Fox suggests.

At times, there's also other software needed or suggested by professors for their course, and that may be free, depending upon the campus. The instructor who teaches the course may provide the software on a class-by-class basis. Ask about the availability of free software in advance of attending the university you choose or during campus visits.

"Other universities offer what they call virtual labs where you may not be able to download the software on your computer, but instead, you can run that software on a laptop in a virtualized environment. That's a new technology. While you can't put the software on your computer, you can connect to a virtual computer that has the software," Fox says.

Help-desk personnel usually don't give specific recommendations for software that students should use for classes, Alex says, but look on college Web sites for articles about suggested specifications for software, computers, and printers. While these articles may not list specific brand names, they will give hardware, software, and printer specifications in a general manner. Such an article is available at its.uiowa.edu. You can search for computer specifications on the top right by looking for "Suggested Computer Configurations for Students."

What are the benefits of having a printer with you on campus?

You can print when you want, what you want, and the way you want—for instance black-and-white, or color to enhance your charts and graphs. No running out in the middle of the night to get something printed at the library or some print shop downtown. Convenience is a blessing.

With your own printer, you have time to experiment with your project. Print out a page, and if you don't like it, make revisions. There's no one standing in line to use the equipment.

Because every workplace uses printers, look at buying one as an investment in your son or daughter. It makes sense because a student with their own printer has more time to master all kinds of tasks with this tool, increasing proficiency, so that by the time they are in the work world they'll be a pro.

For students, some teachers may require those enrolled to print lab assignments or homework before arriving for class. For example, one student had a lab once a week and had to print out the lab before coming to class. If you didn't print out the lab, you received a zero. For a statistics class, students had to print course notes that covered the course lecture and homework before attending class because the students did their homework in class, a Radford University student said.

Often, professors post notes for a specific college learning system in student online accounts, and the student downloads them into a PDF or Word document, added the Radford student.

"While they do have printers at the library, if it's a rainy day or if it's cold, it's a long walk to the library. That's a hassle to do and out of the way, so it's a lot easier to have a printer in your room. I would recommend a printer. A printer is another resource for you to print out research, study tips, or things to help you in college, and it's well worth having one," said the Radford student.

What are some of the drawbacks of not having a printer with you on campus?

Imagine trudging to the library late at night to print something due tomorrow and there are a million people in line. But you need the print project completed now. You think of an academic building with a printer, but it's not open at night. To get something printed, you must put it on your agenda, and even sometimes when you've done that, you can make only so many printouts, or maybe you have a time limit before someone else gets a turn. Being without a printer may also subject you to using antiquated machinery that doesn't have the features you need.

What are some of the drawbacks of having a printer with you on campus?

Some college officials recommend that students don't bring printers, and there's a couple of reasons. The first one is your real estate in your dorm room is small. So, having your own printer just takes up valuable space on your desk. Plus, colleges have wireless enterprise networks, so the printer you may have is a really cool wireless printer. That printer may not work on a university network, and some don't allow printers on the school network. "Students would have to make sure that the printer they could connect to would be via a cable and not wireless. That is the only way they can print," says Laurie Fox, director of educational technology at SUNY Geneseo.

"Another drawback is that toner cartridges are expensive. In some dorms, space is an issue because there might be three to four students in a room. Printers can be large and take up space on a desk or on the floor. Finally, if your printer is malfunctioning, and it's taking up space in your room, that's a hassle," a Radford student says.

Sometimes, having a printer is one more thing to break down, unless you know the ins and outs of disconnecting the machines over school vacations, as some schools require, and setting them up upon return to campus.

A student may want to start out not having a printer to see if it is a hassle getting materials printed elsewhere. This will give a feel for if there's a need for frequent printing.

Are there options for you to get something printed if you have no printer? What are those?

If you are without a printer, you typically can find one in the library, some academic buildings, places where students complete projects in what are known as lab classrooms, and sometimes the student union or buildings with meeting space. Colleges may have a set amount of money they allot per semester for each student on their ID card for a print budget. If you exceed that amount, you'll need to add more money to the card or whip out some cash to pay for copies on-site.

"The library has printers and you do pay by using your student ID. There is money to start on the card when you enroll, but you must supply funding after the account depletes. They do have some printers in a few of the educational buildings, which is a resource that students can use to print documents," says a Radford student.

What are some technical things to think about if you invest in a printer for college?

Start by doing your homework and asking questions of store representatives who sell printers or call dealers. There are typically two types of printers you can buy: a laser printer that uses toner and an inkjet printer that uses cartridges. Here are some pros and cons for each type of printer, according to LD Products.

Inkjet printers
Pros
Less expensive to purchase than laser printer
Good for smaller spaces and lighter in weight
Excel at printing documents with many images, photos, and color documents
Ability to print on different types of paper, including photo paper

Cons

Cartridges don't last as long as a laser printer's

Costly ink

More frequent purchases of ink because they print roughly several hundred pages per cartridge

Slow print speed

Trays hold approximately 50 to 100 sheets

Not meant for heavy-duty printing

Laser printers

Pros

Toner, or ink, lasts longer than an inkjet printer's

Faster print speed — handy when you're printing long papers

Documents have crisper and clearer text

Can handle heavy-duty printing

Cheaper per-page print cost

Each cartridge can print thousands of pages

Cons

More expensive to purchase than inkjet printers

Able to print simple pictures, yet not adept at printing photos or detailed images

Larger in size and heavier in weight

Not as good at printing on different types of paper

Should you avoid having Wi-Fi on your printer? Why or why not? If you do have Wi-Fi, can others use your printer to print?

Don't have Wi-Fi enabled on your printer, especially in the dorm, because with Wi-Fi enabled, other people can send documents to your printer for printing. Most people probably would not want *War and Peace* printed out at their expense — not only the paper costs, but that of toner or inkjet cartridges.

What happens if you have problems with your printer? Where do you go for help?

Ask your school's help desk for assistance. Sometimes, help-desk personnel will come to your room to assist you. Other times, because of coronavirus, they will not. You can also consult with your roommate, or someone on your hall or in your apartment building. Many printer manufacturers also have online technicians to help or toll-free phone assistance for common and not-so-common issues.

"Our school has a technical support system that operates five days a week. Before coronavirus, they would come to your room to help you," says a Radford University student.

What's some advice for getting printers and related supplies? What are some good tips for students?

You can look online for printer supplies near you. Additionally, stores such as Target, Walmart, and your local mom-and-pop shops are most likely less expensive than the bookstore. To save money on supplies, proofread documents before you print them, and specify what pages you need printed rather than printing all of them if that is unnecessary. Use draft mode when printing and try to use Times Roman, Calibri, or Century Gothic text as these fonts draw less ink than the one that sucks up the most ink — the Arial font. Try to purchase higher-yield cartridges to save money — these give your more print pages for your hard-earned cash.

What types of things should you look for in a printer?

Think about what kind of jobs you expect to print, the quantity of print projects you'll have, and the cost of cartridges versus toner. Consider if most of your assignments will involve pictures and few pages of printing text. In that case, go with an inkjet printer. If you are printing out lengthier papers with primarily text, go with the laser printer because it will be less costly overall. You can save money by buying a black-and-white laser printer if you don't routinely do color printing. And for the color printing that you do on an infrequent basis, get that done on a printer available elsewhere on campus.

What kind of computer should I buy?

What are some technical things to think about if you invest in a computer for college? What types of things should you look for in a computer?

The first thing to look at when thinking about a computer for college is what does the college require or recommend?

"Some colleges require you to have a computer. Some colleges recommend you purchase a specific model, and if you do, they will do hardware repair for you, just as an example. Also investigate the college major to see if something is required. Students should bring a current laptop rather than a hand-me-down computer from a parent or a friend," says Laurie Fox, director of educational technology at SUNY Geneseo.

Try to make sure the computer has the latest Central Processing Unit (CPU), and a screen size, battery life, and weight best suited to you. Test drive the computer and see if it's a match for you. If you're in a major that demands a lot of big projects or uses lots of software, go for a larger amount of hard-drive space and RAM, or random-access memory.

In general, purchase new hardware, looking for something lightweight with a long battery. Schools tend to shy away from telling students exactly what computer model to buy because then, if they are not happy with it, Fox hears, "Well, you told me to buy XYZ, and I hate the keyboard." Most colleges give students a lot of autonomy in choosing what they bring.

Be sure to get the computer well in advance of school as many stores could have a depleted supply, and you want to familiarize and use the equipment, plus ensure it's running correctly and set up properly before you get to campus, and that includes installing antivirus software. You'll also want to inquire about computer support services at the university for your laptop in advance of your arrival. The campus help desk can answer your questions about that topic.

To ensure protection of your laptop against damage and theft, examine your homeowner's insurance policy to make sure you have coverage, or purchase renter's insurance. You might also consider a policy that covers theft and damage of the laptop only, with a lower deductible.

Are there advantages to having an SSD drive versus a standard hard drive? If so, what are those?

The term SSD drive means solid-state drive, a storage device. Unlike hard drives, they don't have spinning platters, boot faster, and are not as fragile. Because SSDs are quicker, they aren't as aggressive at sapping energy and, because of that, it extends the battery life of the computer compared with hard drives. However, the SSDs have less storage space and add extra cost to the price of the computer.

Says Fox, "Absolutely there are advantages to having an SSD drive versus a standard hard drive. The first one is speed; an SSD drive is just plain faster. The second advantage is that if you drop your laptop an SSD drive won't crash. Standard hard drives, known as mechanical drives, can fail after a laptop drops on the floor."

Should people in certain majors buy a specific computer? For instance, maybe if you are a photography major you need a computer with lots of memory. Can you think of people in certain majors who should look for certain qualities in a computer? What would those qualities be?

People in certain majors may need to buy a specific computer, and colleges typically do a good job of making recommendations. For example, your daughter may attend a community college for a massage-therapy program, and school officials require her to bring an iPad to campus because all course materials go on that iPad. Specific majors may require a certain computer. For instance, a school of business may generally recommend students in that department buy a Windows computer because it uses certain software only available for use on Windows.

In general, many colleges support both Windows or Mac. But you should check with your school to see if any of the majors specifically say you should have a certain type of computer.

A student should ask an official in their departmental major for information about software or hardware requirements, or technology specifications. For instance, those studying engineering may use more memory and a faster processor because they may use specialized software for classes. For graphic-arts students, you may use Photoshop, which requires more memory than that required for completing word-processing tasks.

Also ask whether to buy a PC or Mac, depending upon the major. While most colleges can accommodate both types of computers, you will want to ask an official in the departmental major for advice on this issue.

Should you get an extended warranty on a computer? Why or why not?

According to the Federal Trade Commission, remember that extended warranties may not cover accidental damage and may only be for factory defects. So, if you drop the laptop on the floor or spill something on it, the warranty may not cover it. But you should know the details of your initial warranty. Know these things:

- How long is your warranty?
- How do you get in touch with the manufacturer for support?
- What does the manufacturer do for you if there is a hardware failure? Do you need to mail them the laptop or do they have on-site repair near you? Will they repair, replace, or refund your money?
- What parts and repair problems does the warranty cover?
- What about accidental damage? Is that covered?
- When using your credit card to purchase a laptop, it may extend your warranty. Call your credit-card company to find out.

As for an extended warranty, Laurie Fox, director of educational technology, SUNY Geneseo, recommends it because at many schools one tiny shop on Main Street does repairs. But with an extended warranty, that gives you peace of mind when you are away at school that you can get service.

Most of the damage on computers at college is accidental damage, often called the "cappuccino test." If you sniff the keyboard and it smells like coffee, you know it's not working because someone spilled coffee. A standard warranty doesn't typically cover accidental damage.

What other computer supplies would you recommend college students purchase? Cables, flash drives, etc.

Some recommended computer supplies include flash drives, which you can carry with you each day, and something you absolutely need. Buy an external mouse and an Ethernet cable to connect via Ethernet, even though most people rely on wireless. When the Internet jams, you will be happy to have the Ethernet cable.

Buy an extra power adapter to have one as a permanent part of your desk, but have another one in your bag or backpack for when you're out. That way, you're not constantly unplugging your power adapter. You can grab the laptop and go.

Having an external hard drive to backup files is important, so you don't lose vital documents, class notes, or presentations. "The external hard drive backs up the computer or you can use a backup subscription to Code42, but definitely arrange for a way to backup the computer. OneDrive is not a backup solution. It is a second storage type of thing. If your hard drive goes, OneDrive just backs up your files, but it does not back up any of your applications," Fox says.

For computer security, you can buy a cable lock. This steel lock goes into a slot or some other type of mechanism on the laptop and then you tether it around a desk or some immovable object to make it difficult for someone to walk off with your laptop.

Make sure your computer has antivirus software installed and running; many colleges require this. Some provide antivirus software for free, so ask help-desk personnel at the school.

Get a surge protector, which protects computers, printers, and electronics from lightning or other electricity issues.

What happens if you have problems with your computer? Where do you go for help?

Most schools have a help desk on campus that's available to students. School staff help with things such as connecting to the network and to printers, and software issues. Some university towns have a small repair shop nearby. Students attending school in a bigger city would obviously have more resources available to them.

What's some advice for getting computers and supplies? What are some good sources for students?

Education discounts for students buying a computer are readily available from major manufacturers. Ask about this at the store where you're shopping and, if you're not in a store, phone customer service and inquire how, as a student, you can save money on the product you plan to buy. You can look for these discounts online as well. Discounts sometimes apply to academic software, so ask about reductions on that.

Don't forget that some universities do have a partnership with computer companies to offer reduced prices. Be sure to ask! Look at your hometown newspapers for sales fliers, which typically come out on Sunday. There, you'll find discounts from big-box stores and major retailers.

Call the university bookstore as well because some will offer discounts on computers and software to students and faculty. During a student's enrollment, some colleges may provide free software and applications, so discuss this with the school's computer help-desk personnel — they are good people to ask.

Administrative

What if you have a learning disability or a hearing or accessibility issue? What services and accommodations are available to you?

What are some of the things you recommend doing if you attend college and have a disability?

In general, it's always important to have updated documentation. You might not know what that means as a student, but reach out to office of accessibility services personnel to see what the university's standards are. Typically, if a student has testing for learning disabilities or a neuro-psych evaluation, the college wants to see adult-age norms. If a student is entering college, that can be time-consuming.

If a student has had testing and has relied on accommodations — and the university relied on scores from when they were much younger at 12 or 14 years old — and the testing didn't use adult-age norms, it's difficult to get them approved in a timely manner. It can be expensive to get new testing done.

"I would recommend if a student is on an Individualized Education Plan or has accommodations in high school, check and see what kind of testing the school has done. Ask for the date for the most recent time the school evaluated them, if that is how their school works. Private schools are a little different in terms of evaluation," says Natalie Ridgway, who coordinates services for the Office of Services for Students with Disabilities at the University of Michigan.

Check and learn those dates, and if the testing is not based on adult-age norms, request new tests. Have the high school do the testing, if you can. That will give you plenty of time and save you money. Around the age of 16 is when they test for adult-age norms.

What kind of services are available to you?

It depends. Services is a large term. The University of Michigan, for example, offers one-on-one academic coaching, which often discusses strategies with people on how to be a more effective student. It is skill development coaching rather than tutoring.

Some schools, like Michigan, have peer study groups and quiet reserved spaces. Depending on an office's funding, students may have access to different technology and software, if it's appropriate. Accommodations are a separate service. Some schools may not offer any of these things, and others may have all these offerings, but offer them each separately.

For instance, some schools may have TRIO, which is a federally funded program on campuses all over, from community colleges to big-time schools. It is an academic advising support service that students can access if they have a disability, if they are from a low-income family, or if they are first-generation college students. An office like that — if it is on your campus and you're looking for extra support — could be a really good resource. This is a service that's not necessarily connected to the accessibility services office.

What kind of accommodations are available to you?

In general, there are two groupings. There are housing accommodations and then there are academic accommodations. Individualized accommodations are based on what the individual's documentation says. Staff consider the accommodations a student has used in the past, and you could also walk into an accessibility office and never need to use accommodations. Sometimes it's a good guide for schools to see what accommodations students have used in the past to see what's necessary for now. The important thing to remember is that accommodations cannot modify essential course content. Some students in high school may have had their tests modified or assignments reduced, but a college would never approve those things. So, there could be some differences, but for the most part, colleges would approve more typical things, such as more time on tests or getting help with class notes.

Note-taking works in a couple of different ways. Sometimes it just means the professor would share more things than they typically would, such as handouts for the student who needs the notes, or the student may have a volunteer notetaker in the class. Depending on the impact of the disability, a human notetaker could be in the class, and that notetaker would sit away from the student to take notes for the student.

Do you have any technology to help students? They even have pens that can take notes.

Yes, those are things that students can investigate on their own and use. Ask if the school has a technology staff member who will meet with students and talk about areas where they need some support. Schools typically have funding for things such as smart pens, note-taking software, iPads, and all sorts of technology. Technology for students with disabilities is important to ask about because that technology will vary greatly depending upon where you go to college.

How about large schools versus small schools — do the larger schools have services that are vaster than a smaller school?

Absolutely. Smaller schools have less funding. Be sure to talk with a staff member in the accessibility services area about technology and what services they can offer you.

What tips do you have when working with an accessibility services office representative?

Just do it. Set up a meeting and get in there. Students and parents make assumptions and follow other guidance — maybe from a high-school special-education department or a physician — and sometimes that information can be helpful, but sometimes there's misinformation about what a college would need and what the life of a student would be like in a university setting. Make an appointment, and you will most likely get the best service by reaching out in advance directly to the office.

See if a staff member can be assigned to a student during the student's undergraduate days. It is helpful to have one person on an ongoing basis with whom the student becomes familiar.

What things should a student do to prepare for a meeting with a representative from an accessibility services office?

If it's an initial meeting, bring to that meeting some general questions and any documentation you have so the representative can look at the information to see if it is outdated or not. Find out how the process differs from what you had in high school compared with college. For instance, if the student had accommodations in high school, some college offices will have the students recertify in their office every year or every semester, so that's important to know. Recertification might mean you need to submit documentation once a year, or it could be that every semester you must notify the accessibility services office that you want to use accommodations, and they will send you a new letter. This is a model some offices use, but it seems like more offices approve you for the whole time you are at the college — depending on the diagnosis — and they will require you to reach out to the office every semester to say you will continue using accommodations or services.

What should you ask when you're seeking accommodations?

Most schools are going to give you a menu of accommodations to choose from. The school is going to rely on you to request what you need. Some things to know that are different from high school are course substitutions. If you have a learning disability in reading and writing, school officials could inquire about getting a foreign-language requirement waived. That is not something that's heavily advertised. Students can request that, and if it's reasonable, they can do that. It would relieve so much unnecessary stress for that population of student. It's also good to look for things like group counseling, especially based on disability groups, like autism or anxiety. Those groups can be a good resource.

How should you get your professor involved in helping you with their class if they know you have accommodations?

Students should go to the professor's office hours. Meet with the professor about accommodations, but don't assume that he has experience with student accommodations. While students are developing their advocacy skills, they may sometimes not know how much to share, what to share, or if it is relevant. If a student can articulate their disability and is able to tell the professor how that disability affects them in the course, that's great. Some students have more complex effects. For instance, some kids with autism may elect to type something out and give it to the professor because that may make them feel more comfortable. Overall, students do not need to overexplain things. They should never have to owe their professor an explanation as to why they have accommodations or why they need something different.

Most accessibility services offices won't release the diagnosis — that's up to the student to do, so the student can decide if that is important for them to do, or if they just want to focus on getting their accommodations met.

For those with mental-health diagnoses, they might choose to say they have unexpected flare-ups at times with their condition, so they don't have to explain to a professor if they have anxiety or post-traumatic stress disorder, also known as PTSD.

There is a difference between high school and college. Representatives from the office of accessibility services will talk to professors if they call that office, but those staff members rarely reach out to a student's professor. It's very much upon the student to make their accommodation needs known, and then professional staff from the accessibility services office can troubleshoot along the way.

Professional staff are available to troubleshoot the situation with the student but, in the end, the student is the one talking to the professor.

Any advice on when you should seek help with your accommodations or services?

Typically, a school will review things once you have applied and accepted. If you're looking at a school, and your disabilities are a big part in that decision, you would start even before that. Sometimes you would start the summer before you go to college.

Students can request accommodations at any time during their college career. The earlier the better. Whether it's getting registered, or you have issues with your services, don't wait. You'll hear every office say that accommodations cannot be retroactive, and that's true. Remember, if you haven't applied for accommodations and services, those accommodations and services can't apply to any past classes you have taken.

What happens if there is a problem with something involving accommodations or services? What would you recommend a student do? Is there anything you can do to alter your accommodations once a professor has signed off on them?

Perhaps you need more time to take tests than you thought, following a math test a professor gave you that had so many problems you couldn't finish it in the allotted time. Talk to your professor if something like that happens. Sometimes office staff can only do so much. Professors can go beyond things that even the office of accessibility services would find reasonable. Start with the professors — especially if the test has already happened.

A student could also go to the accessibility services office and talk about the experience. It could be that the student then receives approval for double the time, if they are having problems finishing tests in the allotted time. In that situation, a change to the accommodation would be case-by-case. Office staff will look for student diagnoses, or if it is a large impairment in one area or another, it is reasonable to see if staff can approve different accommodations.

Any recommendations on what to say when you meet with a professor to discuss your accommodations or services?

Have a straightforward conversation and don't overexplain the disability. In general, let the professor know areas where you have strengths, areas more challenging to you, and concerns about the class. Ask the teacher if there is anything you should know, but you don't need to make a big disclosure during your conversation.

How about a professor who knows you have accommodations, signs off on them, and when you reach out to them for help, they're not so helpful? What do you suggest a student do because they've gone to their professor, but should they go back to accessibility services and say, "This professor is not helping?"

The student should go first to the accessibility services office and their advisor in that office. See what the advisor thinks because they might have some insights and point you to some other campus resources, or the advisor may be able to coach you on how to send an e-mail to the professor.

Many students go through challenges, but they don't reach out to the accessibility services office, and they end up in a bad situation. That does not need to happen.

After reaching out to your accessibility services representative for help, you may also want to try to connect with other students in the class to see if they have some answers to the questions you are having. If there is a teaching assistant, that is a good resource. You can also go so far as to approach your academic advisor and try to transfer to a different section of the class. It may be in a class they know is challenging, such as math or foreign language, and the academic advisor knows another section of the class offers the student better academic support.

What about housing accommodations?

Some schools will do housing accommodations out of the accessibility services office and some schools will do it directly from their residence-life office. You can request a single room, or if you have an emotional-support animal, you would request that through the accessibility services office or residence life. A lot of schools have dorms without air conditioning, and those with asthma can request a hall with air conditioning if they have breathing issues. Some need private bathrooms or semiprivate bathrooms. That's an inclusive list of things that students might request.

If someone receives accommodations and services in high school, are there particular things they should look for in a college from the disabilities services office that might indicate they would have some success? Are there certain things the prospective student should look for?

For the most part, when you are looking at a variety of colleges, most accessibility services offices are going to look similar. They will have the same function; they will be able to approve you for similar things. "Look outside that services office and see what other things the office references, such as programs on campus. I would look for learning communities, TRIO, mentoring programs, clubs based around disabilities — these things will be important to the student. Funding could also be a factor where you see the school gives out a lot of scholarships, which could also be attractive to students. For the most part, you will receive similar support from every accessibility services office. But for the student, it's a matter of what other things you can use, such as those things mentioned above," says Ridgway.

Is it a good idea for someone with a disability to go to a smaller school?

Possibly, but going to a smaller school should not be the number-one thing on your list. You shouldn't say you need to go to a smaller school because you have a disability. It's not the students who are prepared and are thinking about their disability, but it's the students who have invisible disabilities — they've never had services or didn't know services exist. It's students like that who take a long time to find the office of accessibility services.

If you have received services in high school and know you are going to need them in college, those people connect quickly to accessibility services.

What is FERPA? Who should have a signed form on record? How do I access a form?

What is FERPA and when did it come about?

The purpose of the Family Educational Rights and Privacy Act (FERPA) is to protect a student's privacy regarding their educational records. Once a student turns 18 or enrolls in a school past high school, the rights belong to the student. Before that age, the rights to educational records belong to the parents. According to the U.S. Department of Education (DOE), "the law applies to all schools that receive funds under an applicable program of the U.S. DOE."

FERPA came about in 1974 — the same year as the Privacy Act. There was always privacy on the minds of officials.

For a parent to continue to have access to their student's educational records from a university, their son or daughter must sign the FERPA form.

How do I access a FERPA form for my child to sign?

Each institution provides these, and it's not something that the universities and colleges must initiate. Institutions do it in different ways.

For instance, parents come to orientation and the university staff asks the parents, "Do you want to be able to communicate with your son or daughter? Then your daughter needs to sign this form and the school will have them available." Some schools do it that way.

At other schools, you may have to request by asking, "How do I make sure school officials at the institution can have a conversation with me about my son or daughter? Where do I find a consent form?"

A parent may have to call the school if a school did not discuss the FERPA form at an orientation or another event.

When your child signs a FERPA form, what does that give you access to?

The school can give you access to any education records they are maintaining. Education records are records that are directly related to the student. They have the student's name, a parent name, a Social Security number, a student ID, or something that directly links it to the student, and the institution, or a party acting for the institution, maintains it. You would have access to your child's class schedule and grades.

As for medical records, at the postsecondary level the school does not consider them education records unless the records were shared with a nonmedical, nontreatment provider. Then, they become education records. An example of that would be the sharing of a record with an accommodations office at a university; the student had requested appropriate accommodations, and there were records at the health clinic, or a counseling center, which would speak to that request. When those records get shared, they become education records at that point. Under FERPA, the parent would have the right to access those records.

You must think about state law, too. State law affords greater protections regarding FERPA. You can have state laws that take away protection from the students. So, even if the student signs the FERPA consent form, it doesn't mean the institution has to give access. Historically, the college does give access, but the only party to whom they must give access is the student. That is called permissible disclosure.

Can your child revoke the FERPA once he or she has signed it?

Yes. The student can sign the FERPA form one day and go and withdraw it the next. You may ask, "Does the parent have any recourse if the student does that?" They can talk to their child, but the institution has no control over the FERPA form in that situation. The university can only do what the student permits them to do.

What happens if the parents are paying the tuition and their child revokes the FERPA form?

There's another exception that would permit the university to share student information with any parent who claims that student on the parent's tax return. The university does not have to — it's permissible. "I would say half the institutions use the exception, but the other half require the student to provide consent," says LeRoy Rooker, with the American Association of Collegiate Registrars and Admissions Officers.

To find out if a school allows you access to student information after the revocation of a FERPA form, you would generally call the registrar's office with your questions that relate to FERPA. When you inquire with the registrar's office, you would say, "My son is a dependent for tax purposes. I understand there is a provision in FERPA that permits disclosure of education records. As a result, where do I need to provide a copy of my tax return to get those records?" Rooker says. "Then, university officials can tell you they don't honor that or they do."

Is there anything else a student or parent should know about FERPA or the form?

In terms of parental access, rights are always with the student at the postsecondary level. So, for the school to disclose its information from education records to the parent, there must be either a signed, written consent from the student, or it must meet one of the exceptions to signed written consent, which is the dependent student provision.

"The dependent student provision is what we illustrated in the tax return example," says Rooker. "The dependency is based upon the student being declared on the parent's tax return. It's permissible, if the parent provides the tax return, you can white out numbers and that sort of thing. You just need to show that your child is claimed on the tax return with a Social Security number, and it is the current year's tax return. It's important to remember, you must always supply the current year's tax return."

Do you need to file a new FERPA form each school year?

That's up to the institution as to how they want to do it. If the student doesn't limit the form to a specific school year, then the student would not have to file one each school year. But, the university may, as a policy, want the student to sign a new FERPA form each year; however, that is up to the school. It isn't up to the school if the student says you can provide my parent access to the records for school year 2020 through 2021. If the student says that, then the form is not valid beyond that time.

The student can also limit what's provided. The student can say you can provide my parent access to my education records, which gives you academic, disciplinary, and financial information, or the student can give you access to anything. Or, the student may say, you can give my parents access to the financial information. Then, the college has limits on what it can give you. "But not if you come in as a 'dependent student, per signed consent.' Again, that's the one that says if you are claimed on your parents' tax returns, then the school may provide the parent access to education records, and there's no limit on it as long as it meets the definition of an education record," says Rooker.

How does the college health-services area work?

What services are typically available for students at a college health-services area?

Colleges deliver health programs through a wide variety of approaches. Programs range from providing nursing services only to having separate medical, health promotion, and mental-health services, to delivering a full array of on-site integrated primary care, mental health, nutrition, laboratory, radiology, pharmacy, and health-promotion programs.

Some universities offer specialized services tailored to the student market, including travel, dentistry, optometry, physical therapy, and massage therapy. Others offer services for students, faculty, and staff in a unified comprehensive facility. Note that each campus is different and there is a lot of variety regarding offered services due to many different factors. Not all schools have the resources to support a full-service health center. The American College Health Association (ACHA) recommends in its Framework for Comprehensive College Health Program that schools facilitate access to needed services, whether on campus or in the community.

The American College Health Foundation notes that colleges help at the health- services department for injuries and minor illnesses, such as "respiratory infections, gastrointestinal issues, urinary tract infections, and rashes; contraception, well-woman exams, and screening and treatment for sexually transmitted infections; as well as counseling and other mental-health services."

Many health-services areas offer flu shots, and some allow you to show up if you're not feeling well. You can also call and describe your symptoms, including how you feel. They can offer over-the-counter drugs. If you feel bad, you may stay the night at some health centers, so that's an option. Some health centers have an arrangement with nearby hospitals, so they can send you to the hospital if your condition worsens.

What kind of medical information should you have on file with the health-services area?

Many schools will have a health form you fill out when first attending college. Be sure to provide copies of your most recent physical and immunization record to the health-services area, which you can get from your physician at home. Ask personnel at the health-services area how they need the information delivered, and your provider can deliver it to the school by the appropriate method. Sometimes you can hand carry the information to the health-services area once you are on campus. For those with chronic illnesses or severe medical problems, let the health staff know in advance. They will be glad you contacted them.

Be sure to have a health-care power of attorney on file with the health-services group.

Health-services staff will also give you your college medical records if you transfer to another school, graduate, or drop out. These will be helpful to your doctor, so that you don't have any time gaps.

How about kids who are 18 and over and someone who might be 17? Do parents need to authorize medical care if under 18?

"At 18, some states consider you an adult, and the medical records belong to you. In other states, at age 19 or 21 they confer adult status. A good idea is to sign a HIPAA Privacy Authorization Form Health Care Power of Attorney, which authorizes your parents to have access to important medical information," says Rachel Mack, director of marketing and communications, American College Health Association. To find this form, you will go to your insurance provider's Web site, or call them and ask them to send it to you. As a student, keep a copy for yourself and keep it in a file with you at school, give a copy to your parents, and e-mail it to the health center.

Without it, the doctor of a sick student unable to talk and of adult age cannot communicate with parents about the student's medical care.

For those under 18, to receive medical treatment you must sign a consent form. This form should appear on the college's Web site on the health center's page.

See http://www.healthystartu.org/for-students/get-ready/rights-responsibilities/patient-conf/ for more information.

Do you pay with credit card? How are you charged?

Some campuses may charge for an office visit and accept credit cards or cash, or an insurance co-payment. Others bill insurance, and others do not charge for services and, instead, designate a student fee to support health and wellness services. If you have health insurance, be sure to opt out of any plan offered by the school to avoid paying premiums for two plans. You can learn more about different models here: http://www.healthystartu.org/administrators/developing-refining-best-practices-services/revenue-sources-models/.

Does the health-services area accept health-insurance cards? If so, what information does the health-services area need to process a request?

This depends on the school. Some schools require students to have insurance coverage through a family or school plan or the Health Insurance Marketplace. The information needed varies, depending on different factors.

"If you have family insurance coverage, remember to check if health-care providers where you attend college take your insurance. As for a school plan, typically there is a network of services and reasonable expenses to you, plus continuing coverage. The Health Insurance Marketplace may end up costing more and force you to pay more out of pocket, but you can see your options at healthcare.gov/college students," Mack says.

See http://www.healthystartu.org/for-students/get-ready/health-insurance/ for more information.

During visits, health-care staff may request your insurance card or a photocopy of the card, along with your student ID, a Radford University student says.

What do you do if you get sick when the health-services area is not open? Say on weekends or late-night hours?

This depends on what services the campus offers and what services are available in the community. Some schools may use on-call university physicians, advanced-practice providers, counselors, and/or nurses; contracted after-hours medical and/or mental-health advice services; or local university medical school/hospital partnerships to provide after-hours care.

If it's an emergency, many health centers do have a special number to phone. However, if it is off hours and a nonemergency situation, you may need to contact the health-center's staff during office hours, says a Radford student.

What if it's an emergency? What do you recommend a student do?

Colleges typically include information on how to access after-hours services and a directory listing information for local emergency services and urgent care centers on the campus Web site, at campus information desks, with safety and security personnel, and with residence-hall staff.

Is the health-services area staffed by doctors, nurse practitioners, nurses?

This depends on the campus health/wellness service.

How about prescriptions? How does that work at the health-services area?

Not all campus health/wellness services dispense medications or have an on-campus pharmacy. For those who typically take a prescription, before you head to school, ask your doctor to write a 90-day prescription for you, lessening the number of refills. Take the prescription with you.

Mail order is a nice option if you're unable to get a 90-day prescription from your hometown pharmacy. If this doesn't work, you may need to look into a pharmacy benefits package that gives you insurance allowing you to buy necessary prescriptions at your campus residence.

See http://www.healthystartu.org/for-students/get-ready/managing-medications/ for more information.

Some schools may give you basic medications, such as Advil or Tylenol, but for more advanced items, they may send you to a hospital or another facility, a Radford student says.

How about vaccinations for flu, HPV, meningococcal, and hepatitis shots? How does that work at the health-services area?

Many campuses require an up-to-date immunization record and physical before you arrive on campus. As part of your package to enroll in school, you will most likely receive a form for vaccines to fill out and a form for your physical. Give a copy of these documents to health-center personnel, and keep a copy for yourself. Most likely your college's Web site will tell you how they would like the documents submitted.

Be sure to get your documents in on time because many colleges will not allow you to register for classes until you have done so.

See http://www.healthystartu.org/for-students/get-ready/vaccinations/getting-vaccinated/ for more information.

Campus Resources

What about the campus transit system?

Do many campuses have transit systems?

Many large universities have transit systems. Examples include: Texas A&M University; Ohio State University; the University of Georgia; and the University of Michigan.

Are these transit systems typically available 24 hours a day, seven days a week?

Most systems have service every day, but transit systems usually reduce service in the evenings and on weekends. Most systems do not have service that runs 24 hours a day.

Do you pay a per-ride fee, or is there a fee for this service as a part of your tuition or a special student fee?

"Most university transit service is free for all students. Funding for the service varies by university, but some do fund them through a fee charged to all students. In some cities, students may be able to ride the wider transit system for free as well," says Matthew Dickens, senior policy analyst, American Public Transportation Association.

Do the buses typically go to off-campus housing, such as apartments, to pick up students?

Yes, many university transit systems serve apartment developments that house lots of students, even if they are off campus.

Do the buses typically go to grocery stores, drugstores, and stores such as Walmart or Target?

Yes, university transit systems usually serve other places students might want to go, such as shops, downtown, and grocery stores.

Where do you find timetables and bus routes?

The university Web site often has a transportation or transit section that has information on schedules and routes. Many university transit systems now have smartphone apps and real-time information that shows exactly when the bus will arrive at your stop.

Do the buses run during breaks when school is not in session — for instance Thanksgiving, Christmas, and spring breaks?

University transit systems usually run reduced service during breaks.

Are some private buses allowed on campus to take you longer distances?

Yes, as a campus resource, these private companies have buses that use bus stops on campus as a pickup/drop-off spot to take students longer distances. For instance, Virginia Tech does this.

Any tips for using a campus transit system?

Find your university's real-time bus information on its Web site or app to make sure you never miss the bus.

Can you rent books? How does that work? May I preorder books and get them held at the bookstore for me?

Can you rent books on college campuses?

Yes. Books are typically available to rent through a campus store, but that is not always the case. Some stores do not have a rental program. The other thing that comes into play is that there are outside windows of opportunity for students to get their books at places other than university bookstores. As an alternative to the college store — where a mass majority of students may look to rent a book — might be from Amazon or Chegg. While there are a lot of other places to rent a book, those are the two consistent ones outside of a bookstore that have been around for some time.

What is the advantage to renting books versus buying used books or new books?

Usually the cost to rent a book is less than it would be to purchase it, but that is not always the case if there is a used book available. Students may choose to rent a book because they know it's not a subject where they want to keep their book. For instance, maybe the book is for a class they must take versus something in their major. Usually the main factor is the cost and if it is less money to rent the book.

What are the disadvantages to renting books?

If the student doesn't return a rental book, they pay the difference for what it would have cost to purchase that book. Most of the time the campus stores, as well as Chegg and Amazon, send out multiple reminders that a book needs to be returned. Other than that, if the student rents the book and decides the book is something they want to keep, then that's a wash. The only other time a rental book may be less advantageous is if it's for a continuation course. For example, you've taken a course and you've rented the book and you need it for the second semester, but you need to rent it again. Nursing and STEM-type classes typically feature more of the continuation courses.

What are the disadvantages to buying new books?

The biggest disadvantage of a new book is the cost. Other than that, the book has the most relevant content, and it's what the professor has adopted. If the new book is the same version as the used one for a class, you should get the used book to save money.

Are there advantages to buying used books?

Absolutely, the cost is an advantage. As a point of reference, the price difference can be between a 20-percent to a 40-percent difference if you buy a used book versus a new book.

How many students buy used books versus new books?

A research division of the National Association of College Stores called On Campus research does an annual survey of students. The survey receives about 25,000 responses to questions asked on approximately 15 to 21 campuses. The responses are directly from students who answer questions such as where do they purchase their books? In which format are they purchasing their books — for instance, are they buying new or used books? Are they purchasing e-books because that is something you should consider as a growing trend?

"If a student has an option, a student will choose the lowest-cost option almost 100 percent of the time. So, the only time their decision may sway is if it's a physical book — whether that's new or used — or a digital book. The digital book price must be significantly lower than a hard copy of a textbook for them to choose the digital option. Most still want a print book," says Jessica Hickman, vice president of member engagement, National Association of College Stores.

What are the disadvantages to buying used books?

Outside of the campus store, there is more of a disadvantage when buying used books. Sometimes, people will get books from a third-party market. Because of that, you don't know if it's the right edition of the book, if the book is outdated, or if it's the international version, or a teacher's edition.

On other occasions, you'll get a book with tons of highlighting in it, water damage, or pages missing. "When buying used books, you have less control over the quality of the book. However, that's usually not the case if you're buying a used book from a campus store. The campus bookstores do a good job of vetting books," Hickman says.

What are these books with access codes?

Books with access codes are supplemental learning and necessary in some classes to do homework and take tests. Sometimes those access codes get bundled with a physical book. The student needs the physical book and the access code to retrieve the online components necessary for class, such as homework and test-taking. Those access codes could also be bundled with an e-book version, so you get the e-book and the adaptive learning pieces, or the tools to complete different learning components, such as homework and tests.

The e-books are not a new trend. In fact, they've been around for about a decade. "There is a growing movement for faculty to adopt e-books because of the deals representatives from publishing companies may make. If 100 percent of students use the digital version, and have access to digital books and tools, the publisher can negotiate down a price so the students get access to the digital version. If this happens, the publisher is almost guaranteed a sale, and the transaction doesn't contribute to a secondary market for that publisher's books," says Hickman.

Here's how. Hickman adds, "A publisher only makes money the first time a physical book is sold, but when it's a digital book, a publisher always makes money because you can't share or sell a digital book after you have used it. That's why a publisher is willing to negotiate price more for a digital book."

A publisher and a professor may work together to formulate an inclusive access plan where it saves students a significant amount of money when they use a digital access plan. Typically, the bookstore is facilitating this transaction. There are instances where faculty or a university would formulate inclusive access plans, but most likely the bookstore handles these arrangements.

What types of bookstores are there?

There are oftentimes when a division off campus operates and manages a bookstore. For instance, auxiliary services or a business office might oversee it. The staff in the bookstore are staff from the university. Another common model is that universities may choose to outsource that service, so a company like Barnes & Noble or Follett manage the bookstore and employees of the bookstore are employees of that company. In that case, whomever manages that store returns some of the store's profit to the university. The corporation rather than the university makes decisions regarding the bookstore.

What are the advantages to buying new books?

There are oftentimes when no used book is available, and if you don't want a digital book because it is incompatible with a student's learning style — either because of a learning preference or a learning disability — then, in that case, you might buy a new book.

"Honestly, if used or rental books are available — and a publisher may have a different view — always opt for a used or rental book, even if it is a book in your major," Hickman says.

But if a new book for a class is a workbook, perhaps for a lab class where you need to write in it, the preference would be to buy new.

What tips do you have when renting or buying new or used books?

"Compare prices, but always be mindful that you're looking at the exact ISBN. Sometimes, if you search a certain ISBN, search engines will bring you a different edition of the same title. For that reason, the college bookstore on your campus will always have the correct edition and the correct bundles of access codes and books or e-books for you," notes Hickman. Oftentimes, college bookstores have comparison tools, so students can correctly see price differences.

Be aware that sometimes, if you take STEM classes, or if you have a math, science, or foreign-language course, you might find a used book online that does not come with an access code. This is not necessarily a bargain, because if you buy the book, and later find you need an access code for the class and don't have one, you may have to buy another book with an access code — a situation that may cost the student more money.

Buy early, so you have first access to used books.

Make sure a book that's listed as required really is required. Through the National Association of College Stores' research division, one of the other things it does in addition to its survey of students is a survey of faculty. One of the questions it tries to clarify with faculty is when staff may mark a book as required and then the class does not use it.

"When the book is not used in class and a student purchased it, students often get upset about paying the cost for an unused book," Hickman says. "However, the professor looks at this book from the viewpoint that the student should read the book regardless if it is used in class. The teacher may feel the information in the book is not necessarily brought into the lecture or discussed in class, but is still useful for understanding course content."

What is the difference between a recommended book and a required book?

Typically, as a freshman, you buy every book listed by a professor. But the upperclassmen might wait to get their books. That's not necessarily recommended, but the reason they do that is because students have been disappointed in years past when a faculty member never used a required book.

However, students shouldn't wait to get their books because the opportunity to get a used one may vanish. That said, faculty members have the choice to designate a book as required or recommended, and sometimes they make a book a requirement because they feel the student needs to know that information, or it helps them to understand certain concepts, but they will not cover the information using class time.

You have an option to preorder a book, and you're on winter break, but the professor never says what their book is. Isn't that a problem for the bookstore and the student?

Yes, it is a problem, Hickman notes. She says there is something known as HEOA, which is the Higher Education Opportunity Act. Congress stipulated that act be in place to ensure students knew what their expenses would be for classes.

"Usually the bookstore aggregates the adoption information; that is not always the case, but it is most often, Hickman says, "because the bookstore must order the books and then make them available for students. When students register for class, that process is to be complete, so a student can go online to see approximately what they would expect their books to cost them." Now, there are instances where the university has not assigned a professor to a class, so there is no decision about a book for that group of students.

"Faculty members don't understand the true impact on students; they think it is this rule they must follow and don't understand that, by having the information sooner, bookstores have more time to find used books and more affordable options for students," says Hickman. There's also a buyback option at the end of the semester where the bookstore buys back books that they know they are going to need to sell the following semester. If the bookstore doesn't know they need the book, they can't buy it from the student. Then, the student is mad because they are stuck with this book that they thought they could sell to the bookstore and use the money to buy another book.

The books should be available based on HEOA. Even if the students can't order them online before they are back at school, they should have the titles of necessary books, so they can look elsewhere or prepare to look on campus.

May I preorder books and have them held at the bookstore for me? Should you have books shipped to your home?

Preordering books and having them held at a bookstore all depends on the bookstore. Some bookstores call that a reservation program where they will allow for online orders and have those ready and packaged for students. Not all stores do that, though.

You can also preorder books and have them shipped to your house. Another option that some bookstores have chosen is to partner with virtual bookstores. An example of that is a company called Akademos. Akademos handles all the book sales online, so students order their books that way. In some instances, the books would be available to students on campus, or the bookstore could ship them to the student's home.

The bookstores are constantly evolving.

What advice would you give to those trying to sell books back to a bookstore?

Don't just limit your search to the bookstore. The benefit of selling your book to the bookstore is immediate cash. If you sell the book online, you must ship it off to someone and wait for the money to come back. Search for multiple entities to get the most bang for your buck.

Remember, some campuses and student groups will offer opportunities to get books in a different way. For instance, students may look to see if there is an internal way to purchase books. Sometimes students will sell student-to-student and peer-to-peer. There might be a Facebook page for bookselling, and a lot of students learn about that after their first year just because nobody told them about that opportunity. But there are some campuses that facilitate a peer-to-peer selling, such as North Dakota State University, which supports a peer-to-peer selling platform.

There are also companies that set up tents off campus and get the word out that they buy books, and they will give students cash. If the sales fliers say they will pay cash, get nothing but cash. Don't settle for anything less. These companies send word through a campus ambassador, which is a student they pay to share fliers or post in student forums.

Advocate with your faculty and ask to use open resources. It's called OER, Open Educational Resources, and many of those are low-cost print options, or free digital options. An example of a valid company presenting such an option is OpenStax. More professors are adopting books from OpenStax because it's valid and useful information, especially for classes for general education — classes students must take the first and second years before they get into their majors. It's useful to ask professors to seek out these resources for classes taught on topics that don't change, such as geometry or algebra.

Where do I find out about the dining hall hours?

What are the advantages to having a meal plan? Disadvantages?

Practically every on-campus housing plan requires you to have a meal plan, but that is not a bad thing. But if you live off campus in a nonuniversity rented apartment, you may have the choice of opting out of a meal plan. Think about if you are ready to cook for yourself and you have the time and means to do so, or if the cafeteria cooking for you sounds more appealing.

Advantages

It's great not to have to plan for what meal you'll cook, whether you have the right ingredients to make that meal, or the time and energy to cook it. Stroll right on over to the dining hall and, presto, everything's available without lifting a finger. How convenient!

Never worry about eating too much food and stretching your budget for that day to accommodate the unlimited food you can eat at the dining hall.

Once in the dining hall, you are bound to run into someone you know to dine with and socialize. Even better, the dining hall offers a chance to develop friendships with new people or enhance existing ones.

Not having to cook or buy groceries.

Some school dining halls have kosher products, offerings for vegans and vegetarians, and gluten-free choices.

Disadvantages

With your dining dollars, you need to budget. Some colleges have fast-food options with the dining plan, and if you splurge at each meal by eating at the Wendy's rather than the dining hall, you may run out of money before the end of the semester or quarter.

While each campus is different, there may be those schools that don't have a lot of variety in terms of the menu, or which offer no fast-food options whatsoever. When cooking for yourself, you decide the menu.

Do many schools offer a meal plan for those who live off campus? If so, how does this typically work?

There are schools that offer meal plans to those who live off campus. They may offer block meal plans where you have a certain number of meals per semester and you use them as you wish. The dining plan may offer a certain number of meals per week — say 15, 18, or 20 — and you eat at any dining hall when you are on campus.

What are the rules for dining halls in the age of Covid-19?

Most continue dining halls continue to operate, but with some new limitations. For instance, food may be distributed in closed containers, with few self-service options. With staffing restraints, possible lines may occur at peak dining times. Restrictions on table seating often include spacing requirements and sitting with residents of the same dormitory.

What's a person to do if they're an early riser and the dining hall doesn't open until 11 a.m. on weekends?

Plan to have food on hand in the room, such as cereal or breakfast bars, if you're an early riser on the weekends as many of the dining halls don't open until 11 a.m. or so, and by that time, the offering is brunch. At some schools, the dining halls are only open on weekdays. Keep that in mind.

Are there lots of vending machine options on most meal plans? Say you want a midnight snack. How does that work?

Dining dollars, as some campuses call them, allow students to buy things from vending machines, including sodas, candy bars, chips, and crackers. They might be valid at stores designated by the university as providers, such as convenience stores.

What are some ways to maximize your dining-hall dollars?

While schools are different, dining halls typically work the same way. You will pay a certain price for a specific number of meals per week. In addition, you will have money that you can use to buy food at fast-food establishments or stores designated by the university, such as convenience stores. You may also have funds that you can use in vending machines to purchase snacks.

Some colleges will allow you to carry over money to the next semester; others will not have money that rolls over to the next semester.

Dining plans have different types of terms for the money you spend. Some use "flex dollars," which students may use at any dining facility on campus. Other colleges call them "dining dollars" or "swipes."

You will need a meal plan, and it's best to go with the plan suggested by the university for the first semester. After that, you can adjust it based on how many meals you had the first semester, and base future meal-plan purchases on that.

Where do I find out about the dining hall hours?

Each college or university has a different arrangement for dining-hall hours, meal plans, and what is available on their campuses.

Parents and prospective students should locate the dining-services page of the college Web site, where all this information is available, including meal-plan costs, hours, and other locations — cafes, vending, retail — serving food on campus. Most schools require all incoming freshmen living on campus to have a meal plan, says Josh McNair of the National Association of College & University Food Services.

The dining director on each campus is the best person to speak with for more details.

How do I get my mail?

How do I get my mail?

Student mail delivery varies from campus to campus. Students in resident housing should check with the staff for information on correct addressing and other questions about postal services and mail delivery, according to Susan Wright, United States Postal Service Corporate Communications.

At Kennesaw State University students do have mailboxes for their packages and letters, as do many other universities. Says Brenda McClure with campus postal at the university, "With the coronavirus, we have been sending students e-mail notifications to alert them about mail they've received that they must pick up. Since they're not here on campus now, we've been sending e-mail notifications about packages and letters with a cancel notification. If the student calls us or e-mails us, then we will forward their mail to them."

Are there ways to wisely manage your postal budget? What do you recommend?

To save money for mailing and shipping, it's important to note USPS prices appear on usps.com and are not subject to surcharges or other fees — often a surprise when shipping with other companies. For ease of use, Wright says she recommends using the USPS Flat Rate products. Students can mail all items to any domestic address, at any weight, for one low price. Priority Mail provides $50 insurance at no extra cost. Priority Mail and Priority Mail Express boxes, envelopes and labels, and international mailing products and customs forms pouches are available at no charge. Anyone can order these items at usps.com and have them delivered to an address or picked up at a local post office, says Wright.

What types of postal services would college students most likely require?

"Right now, students get all their Federal Express, United Parcel Service, and United States Postal Service deliveries through the Campus Postal at the university. Once school starts again, Amazon will put students' packages in lockers where they also receive packages and letters," says McClure.

"Students can apply for passports at most post offices. This is especially important to students planning to study abroad. To schedule an appointment and find information, go to https://tools.usps.com/rcas.htm," notes Wright.

Whether a care package from home or an online purchase, students are always happy to receive parcel delivery!

The Postal Service is present and active on social media to assist students with questions about anything postal-related. Students will likely be most comfortable accessing information about USPS products and services, or even employment opportunities, using one of these platforms:

Facebook—facebook.com/usps
Twitter — twitter.com/usps
Instagram — instagram.com/uspostalservice
LinkedIn — linkedin.com/company/usps
YouTube — youtube.com/usps

Additionally, the Postal Service app—USPS—is available on Apple and Android platforms. Some of the most popular functions currently available on usps.com include USPS Tracking, Informed Delivery, Post Office Locator, ZIP Code Lookup, the Postal Store, calculating postage, holding mail, requesting Package Pickup, and ordering shipping supplies, which you can find on most smartphones.

What about applying for jobs or internships? What are the most effective ways to reach out to prospective employers by mail?

Priority Mail and Priority Mail Express are effective ways of getting an employment application noticed. "The bright, sturdy, and stately packaging is easily identifiable and studies show the majority of Americans recognize mail as being more personal than using the Internet," Wright says.

What happens to your mail if you're not going to the mailbox to pick it up?

Some students may feel no need to bother with a USPS mailbox because they are not expecting to receive mail. You never know what may arrive, so you should check the box periodically.

Many colleges and universities receive a single delivery from USPS; then, campus employees make the final delivery. Students living on campus should check with the housing staff or campus post office for details about how the university does the mail. In many cases, after 15 days, if you haven't picked up your mail, it goes back to the sender.

What do you do with magazine subscriptions if you only live on campus for nine months? How do you make sure you get the whole subscription for a year?

Says Wright, "We recommend contacting the magazine/publisher directly to ensure a publication subscription is delivered to the correct address. Contact information is found inside the publication itself or by searching online."

What address would you use for absentee ballots when voting? Home or college?

Rules about voting by absentee ballot vary across the country. Students should check the requirements for the state involved.

What about things mailed to you by your family? Do you have any tips?

Here are some tips to avoid a shipping glitch:

- Select a durable box to protect the contents. Priority Mail and Priority Mail Express boxes are free at local post offices.
- Do not reuse boxes — they weaken in the shipping process.
- Properly address packages on one side only and include both "to" and "from" information.
- Print addresses clearly and include all address elements, such as room numbers and directional information. For example, 123 S. Main St., Apt. 2B.
- Never guess a ZIP Code. Look up a ZIP Code at usps.com under Quick Tools. No ZIP is better than a wrong ZIP.
- Place a card inside the package with delivery and return addresses. This helps postal employees deliver the item should the mailing label become damaged or fall off.

- Pay attention to batteries. In general, you should package batteries securely in the manufacturer's original packaging.
- Leave space for extra cushioning inside. To avoid damage, stuff glass and fragile, hollow items, such as vases, with newspaper or packing material. When mailing framed photographs, take the glass out of the frame and wrap it separately.
- Purchase a tracking number from the post office and place it on the package. Keep your receipt in case you want to know the package's whereabouts.

How do I learn about internships?

What are the best ways to learn about internships while you're at college?

The first place you want to start is with your college or university career center because most college career centers will work with students to help them identify opportunities for internships, and a lot of employers will post their opportunities with the career center.

By contacting the career center, students will learn what resources and tools are available to them. Rather than trying to figure out how to find an internship on their own, the university staff can help walk them through the process and make it less confusing and advise students about dates and deadlines for internships.

As for helping students find internships in their major, Mariaelena Marcano said she and others in her role as an internships coordinator at California State University, East Bay know when companies market opportunities that are open.

"Connect with the career center once you get to campus, especially if you are a transfer student. Your time at the college is so limited because you have transferred from one college to the next. The expectation is that you won't be on campus much longer as you finish your upper-level courses and then graduate," she says.

Marcano suggests transfer students work with the career center during the summer they transfer over to their new school, with the mindset that they want placement in an internship that following summer or the following year.

Some schools may organize internship career fairs. These career fairs can be in-person events; however, in the age of Covid-19, these could be virtual career fairs.

When students go to the college career center, what kind of things should they ask?

The professionals at the college career center work on career development with students. For many students, an internship is a part of that process. The questions a student would ask really depend on the student and what point they are at in their college career. For instance, many students may do an internship because they want to explore a field and see if they are interested in pursuing that for a career. Other students may look to an internship to gain some experience in the field they have decided they want to pursue. Others may seek an internship to connect with a specific employer.

"Many employers, especially those who offer paid internships, use those to feed full-time hiring. The employers will typically bring in students in their junior summer and have them work on things. Then, when the students go back to school in the fall, often employers will make a job offer to them for when they get out of school, typically in May or June," says Mimi Collins, with the National Association of Colleges and Employers.

Are there typical requirements of students to receive an internship? For instance, they may need a certain number of semester hours or a minimum grade-point average to qualify?

That depends on the school and the type of internship. You may do an internship for academic credit hours, which your college's academic department sets up requirements for to receive credit.

If you're doing an internship and not receiving academic credit, there are typically employer requirements you must meet to do the internship. Employers can set their own criteria for interns. For instance, they may be willing to serve as the person who supervises the internship for academic credit and signs something attesting that you satisfactorily performed the internship. There may be rules or criteria from your university if you are getting paid or receiving academic credit, so check with a staff member.

It's important to remember that internships are "gray," they are not black and white. Every company is different and has a unique requirement or expectation. "Typical and general internships are the student has a 2.5 or 3.0 grade-point average. They require that you have some type of job experience, or you are involved in a student organization on campus — so some type of leadership role," Marcano says.

Some competitive internships require you to be a senior or postgraduate rather than a freshman or sophomore, so there are two completely different levels of internships. Usually when you look at internships from bigger corporate companies, they examine grade-point averages and want someone who has some type of work experience or a leadership role at a university — for instance they are involved in a fraternity or sorority, student organization, or a part of the student government. There is an interest in seeing how they are involved on campus.

If a student doesn't have work experience, complete service hours in lieu of previously held jobs. For instance, work at a church or synagogue to show volunteer time or do service projects. An employer wants to look at transferrable skills. Additionally, an employer wants to see what story a student is trying to tell on their resume. Even if they lack three jobs with experience and a high grade-point average, what are some transferrable activities that show this student is a viable candidate?

Some companies require letters of recommendation, some ask for a transcript to show the student meets the grade-point-average requirement and attends a specific school during that coming semester. These are basic requirements.

Says Marcano, "I have seen where some companies require students to write a 500-word essay answering question prompts. I have also seen students not get past the first round because they did not complete these requirements during an application process. It's important for the students to be aware of what the requirements are for each individual internship experience because they can all be very different."

Is there a requirement of a sophomore or a rising junior to get an internship?

That depends on the employer and their goals. Some employers will accept students who are freshmen, going into their sophomore year. Others are more focused on sophomores and juniors.

What kind of internships would those be for freshmen and sophomores?

Those would offer entry-level training. Many call these a micro training experience where you don't yet have the proficiency, and you may be entering into your career field and doing more clerical support, introductory level training, and shadowing rather than a junior- or senior-level internship where you receive a project to work on and oversee. There are different levels.

It's important to remember internships also change depending upon the major. For instance, the internship for an art major or a computer-science major would be so different. Usually, freshman and sophomore years involve taking general-education classes with few, if any, upper-level classes geared toward a specific student's major.

COLLEGE, COVID, AND QUESTIONS

The good thing is if you do well in an internship, you often have an opportunity to come back the following year and perhaps work with a different team. That's a way for growth. Some companies have a two- or three-year internship growth program that may eventually lead to employment after the student graduates. This works well because it gives the company a chance to train and vet candidates.

When should you start to look for an internship?

Collins says, "It really depends on the student and their specific goals, but certainly you want to do an internship before you graduate from college." Again, this is where you would want to go to the career center and talk with someone there about why you are doing an internship, what you hope to get out of it, and they can help you find out in terms of timing what might work best for you.

So, for example, you are not sure you want to go into a particular field. You might want to go to the career center as a freshman and say, "I'm not sure about this." They may suggest you try to job shadow or do some type of exploratory experience, which could be an internship.

Or, you're a sophomore thinking about your junior year. The earlier you start the better, but you need to think about your goals. That's why you should head to the career center, so they can at least point you in the right direction.

"Now is the time to start looking for an internship," Marcano says. "When I attend orientations with freshmen and transfer students coming in, I tell them if you have nothing else to do this summer, try and put some work into researching some companies you want to intern with because internships open up during the fall semester for the following summer. That's how typical, big internship programs work — they work one year ahead.

"Part of it is getting ahead of the curve and figuring out which companies you want to apply to during the fall semester for the following summer because you don't want to be the student that walks into the career center in April the following year and you say, "OK, I've decided I want to do a summer internship this summer." By that time, every company has probably selected their candidates for that summer."

Marcano says she tells her students it's not that they won't find a summer internship, it's that the bigger companies you may have wanted to apply to will be in a situation where they can't offer you an internship because the deadline has already passed. If that happens, now you're looking at local companies, some of them smaller, that you may have to call to see if you can find your own placement.

What does shadowing involve?

Shadowing is not an internship experience, but you might go into an organization for a short period of time. It could last a day, or it could be a period of a few days. Often alumni are involved in shadowing experiences. They will have people come in so you can see what they are doing and how it works. While not nearly as robust as an internship, it does give you some idea of the type of work and the kind of environment so, when considering career fields, you have some idea of what to expect.

How can your college or university assist you in searching for an internship?

Again, number one, most career centers collect resources. They can help you prepare for an internship and assist in identifying potential employers and opportunities. Many times, employers will attend career fairs to look for interns. In fact, your campus may have a career fair with employers offering internships there on the spot.

Many colleges do mock interviews, resume review, and professional photos for your LinkedIn and career profiles. They might also assist with career counseling and personality training. Still others offer professional-development workshops to talk about social networking, internships for academic credit versus internships for nonacademic credit, and how to interview, whether it's online, in person, or over the phone.

Other great resources through college are internship informationals, on-campus interviews with employers, and employer panels and panel discussions. Because of Covid-19, schools are also offering virtual job fairs. Don't forget that officials at job fairs may well be looking for interns as well as full-time workers once a student graduates and postgraduate internships.

How would a student prepare for a career fair at school that might offer internships?

Again, this is where a student would go to the career center and talk with the personnel about career-fair preparation. Attire, how to conduct yourself, how to talk with recruiters, the kinds of questions you might need to answer and ask, what to expect, how to put your best foot forward — all those things. There are often some guidelines at the career center they will provide to you, and sometimes they offer workshops on these topics.

What advice is there on doing a university-sponsored internship, which may last a semester?

While some majors require an internship experience, others don't. For those majors that call for an internship placement, students go out and find one, and then they get academic credit to meet that requirement for their major.

There are also students who want academic credit for the experience, so it reflects on the student's official transcript that they had an internship placement. Some companies require your enrollment in an internship class for them to hire you as their intern. Every university has a different process for these internships.

There are also co-ops, which are different from internships. It's a similar type of experience, and co-ops tend to be in more technical fields. A lot of engineering programs have co-op agreements with employers. Obviously, it's a good fit for many students. You must consider how that affects your long-term goals because sometimes co-op programs mean you graduate later because you're working one semester or quarter and in school the next semester or quarter. If your school offers co-op in your field, it's something you would want to explore, so you have a good sense of what's involved and what you can get out of it.

What about the student who wants to seek an internship through their department that they are majoring in?

Those internships are different than if going through the career center. "I would say it's just a different avenue, but typically the same type of experience. A professor may have some insight into the company, but typically an employer that's interested in graduates of a particular school is going to post their internship opportunities with the career center and let professors know about it," Collins says.

What types of things should a student look for in an internship?

It depends on your goals. If you're interested in a paid internship, that will limit a lot of opportunities. For a paid internship, the National

Association of Colleges and Employers' statistics show these internships have many short-term benefits. "Because of legal requirements, employers who pay their interns are permitted to give their interns real work," Collins says. "An unpaid internship can also involve real work, but the employer has to prove the student is getting more out of the internship than the employer."

Collins notes if you're looking to gain hands-on experience, you might want to focus on a paid internship. The other reality is a lot of students can't afford to go a summer without a paid job, so there is that consideration. Students who do paid internships tend to do better initially in terms of job offers, according to the National Association of Colleges and Employers, because often their internship employer will give them a job upon graduation if they performed properly.

"That is not to say unpaid internships are not valuable. They certainly are, but in a different way. Unpaid internships are good for exploration, networking, and reinforcing what you've learned academically. All of those things are certainly positive, so it depends on what you're looking for from the experience," Collins says.

Marcano adds, "First and foremost, seek a layer of mentorship embedded in the experience. Seek a cohort experience and an opportunity to be embedded in the team experience. You also want reflective work where you have an opportunity to reflect on your learning and experiences, either with your site supervisor or with the team. Additionally, you want a layer of networking and professional development. What I mean by networking is being able to have lunch-and-learn meetings with your administrators. With regards to training and experiences, you want layers of learning and training throughout your internship experience. It's not a job — it's a training and an education experience.

"Maybe you've heard something about an internship being free labor. It's meant to be an experiential learning experience," says Marcano. So how do you create those layers of mentorship, networking, professional development, reflection, and community engagement in that experience. How does all this mix into this one experience for the student?

"If a student is reading about a possible internship experience, and it says 90 percent of the work is done independently and 10 percent is something else you do on the job, be cautious of this type of internship," she said. "Because the reality is, they're looking for someone to fill a job. Shame on that company as it is their way of hiring someone at a lower pay scale to complete their work. In fact, it's against the law. The internship experience should be an experience for a student. Companies, by law, should not financially benefit from the work that an internship does. If you read the law, that changes the scope of that experience. It's important to remind employers that this is a learning and training experience for the intern." She said there are California and federal labor laws that apply to interns.

What are some good questions for a student to ask of the person offering an internship?

Number one, before you even get to that point, if you are interviewing for an internship, you need to have done your homework. A lot of this internship information is online. You need to know about the company, so you should have performed some research. Don't ask questions answered in the internship opportunity posting. Assuming the employer does not address these topics elsewhere, you may want to ask what specific duties you would be involved in, who would you work with, and how many other interns would be involved during your internship period? Would there be opportunities to connect with employees? What's management at the company like? What would a typical day look like for the intern? Those are the kind of questions you would ask.

Ask what are some components of the internship? If the company representative says one part of the internship is great mentorship, ask the person if they can talk to you about the mentorship offered to the student. What does the mentorship look like in this experience?

When you speak to the interviewer, if this information did not appear online or with an internship application, ask these questions:

Is it a paid internship?
Is the internship for college credit?
Is this a virtual internship due to Covid-19?

Can this internship lead to a full-time position at graduation? If so, what is you track record of hiring interns for permanent jobs? Is there someone who was an intern, who now works for you full-time, that I could speak to?

If the internship description mentions networking, ask if they can tell you a little bit more about networking opportunities for this internship. By asking these questions, it drills down into whether they offer things like colleague and internship lunches, weekly team meetings, competitions between teams, and it has them give examples of what they do.

When you ask clarifying questions about their internship, it's helpful to see what that experience looks like, and what it will be like if you get the internship.

As for career fairs where representatives from different companies may offer internships, if it is a company you've had time to research or a firm you're meeting for the first time at a job fair, walk up and introduce yourself. Have a resume ready to give to the representative, and tell them you are interested and you would like to know more about their internship experience. That shows that you are taking the first step of advocating for yourself in your career journey. If you are the quiet person in the back going from table to table, who will know you that day?

Part of it is stepping out of your comfort zone — whether you are an introvert or extrovert — and introducing yourself. Second, depending upon what's said, try to find out what the timeline is for those internship opportunities. Every internship has a deadline as a part of the process. Put that information on your calendar, because if you don't do it at that time, you're probably not going to do it later.

Finally, go to career services because the people there can offer specific, deeper, and richer guidance.

Are there any drawbacks to having an internship?

Usually not, but there are exceptions. What would be a possible drawback to getting some experience? "Remember that getting coffee for a boss and photocopying papers for higher-ups doesn't qualify as an unpaid internship because it does not meet the FLSA (Fair Labor Standards Act) standard for an internship, which is: in order to offer an unpaid internship — and it's hard for for-profit employers to offer unpaid internships — they have to prove the student is getting more out of it than they are. So, what am I getting out of it if I am making coffee? I'm getting nothing," says Collins.

For instance, if you think of someone who student teaches, that is not a paid internship, but part of the coursework. You're getting academic credit for it, but you're doing real work. You're in front of a classroom, you're working with students. You're learning how to handle a classroom. You're learning how to handle subject matter. That's a real benefit to the person doing that experience.

COLLEGE, COVID, AND QUESTIONS

There are no drawbacks because internships are an opportunity to test drive your career. It is an opportunity to look through the lens of your career field and see if this is the area you want to move in to. Many times students go into an internship noting they want to be in a particular area. However, that internship opens their eyes to another career area because they see the inside workings of an industry in a different way. It gives you a chance to pivot a different way and go in a different direction to see another area that you'd like to learn more about. And it also gives you the ability to change your major because you've learned that work is not for you.

For people working a job to put themselves through school, it may be hard to give up that job to go to a part-time internship that is temporary. However, Marcano says, "You don't want to be that senior with that part-time job that is not connected to your major in any way. Because now you've graduated with a degree, and you're applying for jobs in your major and people will ask you what kind of experience do you have in this career field? Being able to show transferrable skills is real."

It takes a lot of work to find an internship, but this is a skill set that shows you are passionate about the work that you do. It shows you're persistent in wanting to work in that career field and in getting and obtaining what you want.

"You are also getting the job done and willing to adapt to an ever-changing environment. National studies have shown that employers are looking for that type of person. Having these experiences under your belt really speak to who you are as a candidate," Marcano says.

Regarding the downside of internships, it does take a lot of work. The early bird gets the worm, and it takes work to find the internship. It's typical that you don't get the first internship you apply to. "We typically tell our students, apply to 10 to 20 internships, and let's hope you get a call back for five of them because competition is fierce," Marcano says.

When Google says it gets 3,000 applicants and can hire 200 interns, you know that competition is fierce. But once you're in as an intern, you have a high chance of retainment as an employee — unlike taking a part-time job that is not in your career field that is not helping you develop the skills for the career field that you want to be in.

What are the positive things about having an internship?

There are lots of positives to having an internship. It can help you confirm your career choice or help you determine that is not the professional path for you. It gives you some experience in the field. You may be able to develop a professional network through an internship. It will give you a leg up on students who have not done internships. Employers look at that as a positive sign.

Most students don't have real work experience. An internship is the closest thing you can do to match real work experience. That's important, especially in the case of paid interns, because it can be a foot in the door with a company.

Being able to learn about your career field and specific projects within that field; learning platforms and technology used currently; and the experience of working in your field are all positives. By test driving your career through an internship, you can find if that is the right fit for you.

The other piece is having a mentor. That mentor is the site supervisor during your internship. The idea is for that person to not only mentor you through that experience, but now you have a connection on a professional level that hopefully will continue past that internship experience. The idea is you're going to receive a job offer or possibly get a referral or letter of recommendation to your next opportunity. Letters of recommendation can help you build your career.

You need to take the risk of doing the work to find an internship and doing well in your internship. Don't be the mediocre person that just does what they are told. Maximize every experience you have and network with the people that are there. Go out to lunch with your team. In the coronavirus environment we are now in, do online networking, and ask your supervisor to connect you with someone that you can reach out to online. You can connect with these people on LinkedIn, which then allows you to say, my internship is ending soon, if you have any suggestions or leads, please let me know. Reaching out to that new network might provide you with a new opportunity.

Internships open opportunities that you would not normally have.

What happens if you try to get an internship and don't succeed?

Marcano suggests working with your school's career center to see if you can work as an intern with a small company. "Let people know you are a student at XYZ school studying and name your major. Can I do a project in this area for your company? Usually, finding an internship is student-driven," she says. The career center provides students with the tools and the resources on how to find the internships.

How can a school's alumni network help you get an internship?

Often the career center will work with alumni services and help students connect with alumni who are either in companies offering internships or, sometimes, alumni are involved in job shadowing. Alumni can help with networking. Those are a few ways alumni can help.

Depending on how strong your alumni association is, the alumni association, career center, and development office have a partnership. Getting companies and alumni to participate in professional-development panels or creating pipeline opportunities to careers at companies can be helpful.

What about LinkedIn where you can sign up as a student and post your resume? How have employers used that?

LinkedIn is social media, but it is more about being a professional, unlike Facebook, where that is for personal use and LinkedIn is for professional use.

Is there a resource where a student goes online and career services can help them locate an internship?

Most colleges and universities have a career platform. For example, some universities have Handshake, Symplicity, or GradLeaders as their professional job platform. They are job platforms like LinkedIn, but on a college level. Because the universities usually contract out with this platform, that's why it's more important than ever to connect with the career center. The career center will let you know what platform the college uses and how to enroll, and how to craft your resume and profile before uploading it, so that you can be a viable candidate.

Depending on the profile or the platform, each platform may determine what's an active profile differently. For example, there are some that say if the student's name is input and they have nothing in their student involvement section — they haven't gotten involved in any campus activities — but they have all their job descriptions in place and their job history, then that one category being empty means that profile is not complete, which means an employer cannot see that profile. It's important for the student to have a complete profile, so you need to learn from university officials what constitutes a complete profile.

The companies, such as LinkedIn and Handshake, pay money to gain access to student information because these students are possible future employees. But they are only going to receive completed profiles from the university, so the companies may miss finding out about a great potential candidate just because the student didn't complete their profile.

That's why LinkedIn is so adamant about having a complete profile. If you don't have a complete profile or you're not active on your profile, employers are going to search whose been active most recently and who has a completed profile. Why would an employer waste their time on someone who doesn't have a complete profile? Without a complete profile, it makes it difficult for an employer to gauge if they have a good candidate sitting in front of them.

Are there other ways to apply to an internship?

Some companies offer an online portal where you submit an application to a prospective employer.

Roommates and Residence Life

What should I bring to school?

What should I bring to school?

The first thing to do is to find out the size of the room because rooms are modest in size, and sometimes three or more students are housed in one room. For that reason, don't bring too much. In fact, before you start your packing list, find out what the school provides.

Next, check the residence-life section of your university's Web site, where school officials will most likely list what you should bring, what you should not bring, and what the school will supply in the room. The school may also mail or e-mail you a list of what to pack. For move-in, use a hand-held folding luggage cart, a dolly or hand truck, and bungee cords to strap your items to keep them from falling.

What school supplies should I bring?

Top of the list are a laptop computer, charger, printer, Ethernet cable, USB cable, mouse, portable charger, backpack, lanyard to hold student ID and keys, and a smartphone. Two important apps to have loaded on the phone you own are Find My iPhone or Google's Find My Device for an Android phone. Venmo, which you can use to pay people and get money from them by using an account associated with a credit card, a debit card, or a bank account, is a good app to install, too.

You will also want a surge protector for your electronics and an external hard drive to make sure you have important documents copied onto this device. Yes, iCloud, Google Drive, and Dropbox are available to store files, too, but at some point they cost money if you exceed the free storage limit.

You can also watch Netflix or Hulu from your laptop to avoid bringing a television.

As for supplies, noise-cancelling headphones, headphones, or ear plugs; extra-long cables; graphing calculator; duct tape; desk lamp; ruled notebook paper; binders; folders; erasers; spiral notebooks; highlighters; pencils; pens; pencil sharpener; envelopes; stamps; paper clips; index cards; Post-it Notes; stapler; rubber bands; colored pencils; colored markers; flash drives; three-hole punch; reinforcements to repair lined notebook paper holes; scissors; toner or inkjet cartridges; ruler; glue sticks; tape; dictionary; thesaurus; *The Elements of Style* (Strunk and White) grammar book; school planner/agenda; a flashlight and batteries; and a desk organizer with slots to put various supplies — pens, pencils, highlighters, paper clips, etc.

To find out if there are any student-discount cards or discounts available to you as a student, type in "Student Discounts (followed by current year)," and maybe you will be able to save on school supplies or other goods for your dorm or apartment.

What types of clothing should I bring?

Wherever you go, look at the typical weather in fall, winter, and spring. That way, you'll have the best idea as to what to bring. Suggested items include the following:

Umbrella, raincoat, and snow boots; gloves and hats; winter coat; tennis shoes; casual shoes; dress shoes and dress shirts and ties; belts; flip-flops; pajamas; jeans; long-sleeve and short-sleeve shirts; pants; shorts; sweatpants; sweatshirts; jackets; socks; underwear; bathrobe; and workout clothes.

For women, you might want to bring casual jewelry; purses; flats; leggings; yoga pants; casual and date dresses; and skirts.

For job interviews or sorority or fraternity functions, have a nice dress on hand and a dress shirt, blazer, belt, and tie, along with appropriate shoes.

What room furnishings should I bring?

If your dorm has no air conditioning, bring a fan, but coordinate with your roommate, so you both don't bring one. Other items needed include: a broom or vacuum; family photos and pictures of friends; dry-erase board for your front door; wall art or posters; for use in the bathroom and room, use suction hooks, or adhesive hooks and strips that allow you to take them off without damaging the surface. Don't forget the alarm clock.

As for bedding, check with residence-life officials to ask the size of the mattresses because many are not standard twin-size. For many dorms, you will want to bring two sets of extra-long twin sheets and pillowcases; two sets of bath towels, hand towels, and washcloths; a bath mat; a shower curtain and an inner liner (coordinate with roommates, so you don't have more than one) a pillow; a mattress cover; an egg-crate mattress pad or type of mattress topper; comforter; fleece or thermal blanket; a big pillow to prop up or a bed-rest pillow to sit up in bed and study; hangers; bed risers, if the school allows them and some colleges do supply them. Be sure to bring some under-the-bed boxes to store extra bedding, sheets and towels, school supplies, and toiletries.

What types of laundry and toiletry supplies should I bring?

In case you must walk down the hall to use the shower, it's helpful to have a plastic pail or shower caddy to carry your items as well as flip-flops to travel there. Here are some other items to bring as toiletry supplies and to do laundry: coins, if your machines are coin-operated rather than using a swipe card or student ID; soap with a plastic dish; deodorant; shampoo and conditioner; toothpaste and toothbrush; floss; lip balm; razors and shaving cream; combs and brushes; skin lotion; hair products; hair dryer; curling iron; makeup and makeup remover; nail polish and nail polish remover; tissues; Q-tips; cotton balls; sunglasses; glasses and contacts and related cleaner, and maybe a backup in case you lose them; VISINE; pain relievers; cough drops; a first-aid kit with Band-Aids; prescription medicine; aspirin; tampons or pads; nail clippers; nail file; toilet paper (check with your school as housekeeping staff on campus may supply this after the initial first week of school or so); detergent — liquid or powder, and if washing by hand, Woolite); laundry bag; drying racks; delicates bag; and fabric softener.

How about things to keep the room clean?

Paper towels; trash bags; toilet-boil cleaner; Lysol; air freshener; carpet cleaner; a trash can for room and bathroom; and dust pan and broom.

Any things you shouldn't bring?

Start first by looking in the material that the school sends you and by visiting the residence-life Web site, where school officials typically list what you should not bring. If there is no list of what not to bring, call or e-mail residence-life personnel. The list of things not to bring should include electric blankets; space heaters; halogen lamps; pets; water beds; candles; toasters; toaster ovens; griddles; slow cookers; grills; hot plates; broilers; electric frying pans; anything related to high school, such as your yearbook; guns; furniture, expensive clothes, and jewelry; a car; fireworks; dry-clean-only clothing; glass items, such as cups; and ceramic items, including bowls and plates.

What tips do you have for organizing your things and getting them into your dorm room or apartment?

Get a large box, and start putting in your linens, school supplies, toiletries, and miscellaneous. In another box, put your clothes. In another box, put your kitchen supplies and food. You can put appliances and room decor in your final box.

What kitchen supplies if living off campus?

Bring paper plates; dishes, mugs, cups, utensils, and bowls — all made of plastic and preferably microwavable; can opener; food storage bags; measuring spoons and measuring cups; sponges; dishwashing liquid; dish strainer; coffee machine; and ice tray.

Food supplies?

Cereal; granola bars; crackers; peanut butter; macaroni and cheese; popcorn; sodas; snacks. Store food in bins with lids. Bring paper plates and utensils and bowls — both made of plastic and preferably microwavable. A can opener and food storage bags.

Miscellaneous?

If you have a car on campus, be sure to bring a copy of your insurance paperwork and a photocopy of your health-insurance card. Store these documents in a safe place.

A bike and bike lock and a bicycle pump to pump tires.

What do schools provide?

Before you start your list for what to buy or pack, contact the school and ask them for room dimensions and what the rooms look like. Most colleges have photos of the room and some have virtual tours featuring dorm rooms. Ask if the rooms have carpeting and air conditioning.

You will find that most dorms have kitchens with refrigerators and microwaves, plus essential items to make things, such as utensils, measuring cups, pots, and pans. Rooms have Internet, and usually a bed, dresser, and a desk. There's also a closet for each student.

Many colleges allow you to rent at school dorm room mini refrigerators, microwaves, and carpeting.

How do you recommend working with your roommate to coordinate what to bring?

After you've found out what the university does and doesn't provide, call your roommate and discuss the information you learned from the school's housing office. In this way, you can make sure you bring what you need and don't have duplicate items.

The parents of the roommates should also be involved so they have contact information for one another, such as cell-phone numbers, home phone numbers, and e-mail addresses, just in case there is an emergency among roommates. It's also a great way for the parents to share this milestone of their students being in college together.

How do I protect my belongings?

Can I afford to replace my lost or stolen items?

If not, consider insurance. There are a lot of types of insurance available. Some insurance is for people living in dorms, which has lower premiums. As an alternative, there is insurance for those renting off-campus housing, including apartments, which generally have higher premiums. Be sure to research your options.

What kind of room insurance is available to me? Any advantages to having this insurance? Any disadvantages to having this insurance?

If you're going to live independently for the first time, what property do you have and can you pay for the damage? As an example, there are 2,000 fires reported in dormitories every year, says John Fees, co-founder and managing director of GradGuard. These students leave candles on, they hit a sprinkler accidentally, they leave clothes on a sprinkler.

"If a sprinkler goes off, the average damage is about $60,000. Everybody's computers on that floor are ruined. That student who caused the fire is responsible for paying the damage costs," Fees says.

One of the reasons renter's insurance is important is if you can't afford to replace the property you damaged, schools will hold you responsible for that.

And if you can't afford to replace your stolen backpack, beware. At the University of Kentucky in 2017, Fees says, 70 backpacks were stolen in the first week of school. What's in a backpack? A $1,000 computer, a $700 tablet, three books that are worth $300 each. Every backpack is worth about $2,000 to $3,000 to a drug dealer on meth looking to feed a habit. So students are an easy target. Renter's insurance for about $11 or $12 a month is one of the easiest and smartest things to buy.

Fees said his company GradGuard, has created insurance products to protect more than 700,000 families and has paid thousands and thousands of claims, getting people through big setbacks.

What are the risks to living on campus?

For many of the nearly three-million students who live in student housing, they need to remember that there are an average of 2,000 fires reported annually within on-campus housing by the Clery Act, a crime and safety database, and 69,502 property crimes stated in FBI Uniform Crime Reports. So, the risks are real. It is also important for families to realize that a 2020 survey revealed that 65 percent of the top 20 home-insurance providers do not provide coverage to students living in student housing, says Fees. Homeowner's insurance may also not be practical due to coverage limits, high deductibles, and the increased cost of your insurance if you file a claim. There is college renter's insurance, however, that provides a low deductible and coverage designed for college life, making it a must-have consideration for families.

What does renter's insurance cover?

Theft, vandalism, fire, and natural disasters, including hurricanes, are the typical things covered. If a fire forces you to live in a different location, then the policy may also may pay for what it costs to reside somewhere else. The same is true if an injury occurs to a guest while at your place, the insurance may cover the liability. Floods are not covered.

What information do you need to file a claim?

For renter's insurance, the most important thing the student should do is take pictures of receipts of property they own as well as photos of those possessions. If your bike gets stolen or someone takes your backpack, call your insurance company. Most likely, they will ask you to send a copy of the receipt and reimburse you with a check. Some of those insurers will replace your product with the same quality you had, not the depreciated cost.

If there is a fire on a university campus and the dorm has a lot of damage, the insurer sends a claims adjustor to the campus, and the students who are affected will get paid through insurance. On the other hand, if a student sets a sprinkler off, instead of paying everyone for the damage, the university will replace everyone's computers, pay for the damage, and file a claim on behalf of the student, Fees says. Basically, if a student damages other people's property, the university gets involved and makes the claim to make sure all students receive fair treatment. The student doesn't have to worry about paying all the people.

How about auto insurance while at college? What should a student know?

Unless you need a car for work, many insurers generally recommend to college students that they should use ride-sharing services for campus living. "The total cost of car ownership when you include the cost to insure college-age drivers makes it an expensive proposition to have a car on campus. However, if you do need a car, then make sure you don't just purchase minimum coverages. If an investigation finds you responsible for a car accident that you cannot pay for, it could mean that your future income could be directed to pay for the damages you may be liable for," says Fees.

Visit https://mylifeprotected.com/auto-insurance, which provides quotes from the major insurance companies and will also help you to identify if you may qualify for a "good-student" discount — you could save five to 15 percent! Another important factor to recognize is that the cost of your auto insurance may be higher if you have a low credit score. Though some states prohibit the use of credit scores, a low score can also cost you more money on your auto insurance.

Are you still covered under your parents' family health-insurance plan?

Doublecheck this with your parents. By law you can, but not necessarily, remain covered until age 26 on their policy.

How about health insurance while at college? What should a student know?

Many colleges offer health-insurance plans to students and require them to purchase or opt out by showing proof of alternative insurance. According to the American College Health Association, about 10 percent of students get their health insurance through their school. A college health-insurance plan may make sense for some students. But if you have family health insurance, your college student can remain on a parent's plan until the age of 26. Be sure to confirm the requirements to use your student campus health clinic, and be certain not to pay twice for coverage.

The students have gone through the admissions process and selected a school. Going to college pays off for most people. But it only pays off if you graduate. "25 percent of students who started in 2017," Fees says quoting Department of Education statistics, "did not reenroll anywhere for their sophomore year. Then you look at it in the context of 60 percent of students don't even graduate in six years. When you're spending about a quarter-million dollars, for an education, it seems a bit of a risk. You must ask, "Well, why is that?"

"Part of it is this generation," he added. There are a lot of factors influencing this: health reasons and substance abuse are the primary ones. One of the main messages for those students living on their own for the first time is to take care of their health. Their health will keep them well enough to complete their degree." That may sound obvious, but in the time of Covid-19, it is even more important. Taking care of yourself, eating, and sleeping right are so important.

What about tuition insurance coverage? What should a student know?

The other thing that students aren't aware of this — you may not know what the refund policy of the school is. Covid-19 has brought attention to that, but most schools don't provide a refund. "If they do provide a refund, it's only for a prorated amount of the tuition you paid. It doesn't include the deposit, it doesn't include the room and board, it doesn't include the academic fees you might have paid," Fees says.

So if you can't afford the costs of an extra semester, you might consider tuition insurance that does provide a refund when school's out. It works a lot like travel insurance. It's affordable. About $8,000 worth of coverage is about $6. So, again, it's usually less than about $15 a month just to have coverage that will help you recover money from your academic term.

If your student must withdraw from college due to a serious illness, injury, or accident, it is unlikely that you will receive a 100-percent refund. Fees says, "Only six percent of schools surveyed in 2019 provide 100-percent refunds of tuition, and virtually no schools will refund the cost of academic fees, room, and board." Tuition insurance can provide a refund, however, when schools do not. Bottom line is it is important to know your school's refund policy and to be aware that you could lose all the money you invested in tuition, academic fees, room, and board. If you cannot afford the cost of an extra college semester, then you might consider purchasing tuition insurance coverage prior to the start of classes.

College is a great investment, but it is not risk-free.

Do the university police provide engravers to mark my belongings?

Do the university police typically provide engravers to mark my belongings? How does that work?

Some schools offer — either at orientation or during school sessions — workshops about campus security. Engrave belongings of value, and much of the time you can visit the campus police office to borrow for free an engraver and use it at the facility to engrave your items.

Keep a record of the serial numbers, make, and model of your belongings. This includes phones, cameras, musical instruments, laptops, printers, and large trunks of clothes and shoes.

Some of the schools providing engravers include Duke University, Allegheny College, and Radford University. Duke offers a program that allows the campus police to engrave student's valuables with an ID number placed on belongings for tracing purposes. At Allegheny, officers come to residence halls and sites on campus to engrave items, with students receiving a sticker for "Operation Identification" for their dorm room or residence to note they have engraved items. The police department at Radford offers engravers to students who stop by to engrave their items at the campus facility.

Any suggestions from the campus police on how to keep someone from stealing your possessions?

To keep track of what you own, write down serial numbers for personal items, such as laptop computers and electronics. File that information someplace safe. For those things of value without a serial number, use an engraver and put your driver's license number on the items. During school breaks, bring home expensive items.

Lock your dorm room, even if you know you will return soon. Mark your textbooks by choosing a private identification number known to you and listing it on a page. That way, if it's sold to the university bookstore, you have a way of identifying the book.

If you live off campus, use an automatic timer for some of your lights to make it look like someone is at home. Keep your windows and doors locked for your apartment, and be sure to roll up your windows and lock car doors.

Any recommendations on how to stay safe on campus — whether it's you personally, your belongings, or your car?

When you shop, don't bring lots of cash. Be aware of your purse, and better yet, use a fanny pack or a clutch purse. When shopping in the evening, try to go with someone and complete your trip before dark. Use parking spaces near a light and preferably close to the store. Store anything of value in the car's trunk. Many stores have security staff who will walk you to your car; be sure to ask store personnel. Park away from cars with windows that are darkly tinted. Be aware of your surroundings, and alert staff if someone trails you in the store or to your car. Go quickly to your parked car.

Avoid visiting the ATM late at night.

Try to walk with a friend on campus, and ask for a campus escort to bring you back to your dorm room if you are out late on campus. Let your roommate or a friend know by cell phone when you are heading back to your dorm. Many campuses have emergency alert systems on a lamppost at various locations. You can press it to alert school security about a concern or call for help.

How do I move in?

How do I move into a residence hall? What steps would you follow?

Each college has its own process for moving into a residence hall. Most schools have guidelines in place and specified days when students can move on campus. The Covid-19 pandemic has muddied the waters even more as schools attempt to spread out their move-in windows to maintain social distancing and limit the number of moving trucks that can be on campus at any one time.

Be sure to collect all relevant information from your school's student-affairs office before rolling up to your assigned residence hall. Generally, the smart move is to move in as early in the day as possible — before the parking lot and hallway crowds get too big — and then escape to get lunch and tour the campus before returning to unpack and organize in the afternoon once the commotion has settled down.

Any advice on the best way to get my stuff into the dorm or apartment?

How much do you have to move? The amount can vary a lot due to the size of the room or personal preference. This can dictate how much planning or assistance you will need. Remember that with Covid-19, a reservation time slot for a dorm move in may be necessary.

Your budget will largely dictate how you handle the move. If you're on a tight budget, it's probably up to you and maybe a roommate, your parents, or some other friends on campus to get your belongings inside the residence hall. If you're transporting your belongings to school, a 10-foot moving truck — the smallest in the U-Haul® truck fleet — is usually perfect for students. It can easily fit a king-size bed frame, dresser, mini fridge, bicycle, and plenty of boxes. It's also small enough to park on campus and easily maneuvered throughout campus roundabouts and tight turns. Find a full selection of equipment on uhaul.com.

"If you're seeking the white-gloves treatment," says Jeff Lockridge, manager of media and public relations with U-Haul International®, "the "Ship to School" option offered by Collegeboxes® is the ultimate hands-off solution. Powered by U-Haul since 1999, Collegeboxes is the No. 1 student storage and shipping provider in the country." With Ship to School service, students don't have to load and drive a moving truck, or lug large suitcases and boxes to the airport. Everything ships straight from your home to college, and Collegeboxes works directly with residence-hall officials to deliver your items to your room before other students even arrive on campus. Create an account and do some pricing on Collegeboxes.com, and you may find the ease of this stress-free approach is well worth a few extra dollars.

Are there typically people to help with the move in?

Some campuses offer move-in helpers, some of whom are upper classmen or second-year students, so it's a great way to meet new students. Other colleges and universities do not provide physical assistance with the move-in process. For students who could use some moving help when the roommate or parents can't be there, the simplest solution is MovingHelp.com. This is a Web site where you can hire local Moving Help® Service Providers by the hour. You select the number of people needed, the date, time, and hours you need them, and then choose from the available options based on customer reviews and price. U-Haul® powers this online marketplace for local moving companies and serves as the third-party oversight, holding the customer's funds until job completion and the customer okays the release of payment.

Any packing tips?

Pack larger items that you won't use right away at the bottom of boxes. For more significant and commonly used items, pack those in smaller boxes that are easier to unload.

When in doubt, label it. You should label every box, bag, and bin. You can write directly on the box, or write on a piece of tape if you are planning to reuse the box. Labeling your boxes will make the unpacking process quicker and smoother. It feels like an extra step, but you will be grateful when you arrive at school and are trying to find your laptop.

Also — and this applies to incoming freshmen — you don't want to move everything you own to school. Identify what truly must go with you, and the rest can stay at your parents' residence. Once you start packing, remember that a full box is a secure box. But keep the weight below 30 pounds to prevent crushing.

Keep your toiletries, clothes to wear during the move and once you arrive, and other daily-use items easily accessible. Cleaning supplies, sanitation wipes, and vacuum and broom for your new residence should be among the last things you put on the moving truck or other mode of transportation, so they can be the first things unloaded.

Any types of boxes, dollies, or packing supplies you recommend?

The most helpful item you can bring to any move is a traditional utility dolly or hand truck, or a foldable luggage cart. "A utility dolly can be placed in the cargo area of your U-Haul® truck rental for just a few extra dollars, or you can rent one on its own. This little lifesaver can help you avoid days of back pain, or a potential accident, while also minimizing the number of back-and-forth trips from the vehicle to the residence," Lockridge says. If you have large and especially heavy items, a furniture dolly or appliance dolly may be worth adding to your checklist.

Furniture pads are a wise and cheap purchase if you have nice furnishings that you'd like to avoid seeing scratched in the cargo area of a truck or trailer. Bubble wrap, packing paper and/or packing peanuts are necessary if you have dishware, mirrors, and other breakables. "U-Haul offers a 100 percent box buyback guarantee for any boxes you purchase and don't use, as long as you have the receipt. So, don't worry about buying too many boxes — and you typically need more than you think. U-Haul also sells specialty boxes for wardrobes, flat-screen TVs, and many other household items," Lockridge says.

Any specific tips for moving into an apartment?

While some residence halls offer elevators and indoor entry to rooms, most apartment complexes — on or off campus — do not. And if you have not secured a ground-level residence, you will be climbing stairs and probably maneuvering around some tight turns and walkways. Keep this in mind, as the need for physical assistance (MovingHelp.com) or lighter boxes becomes even more necessary. Fortunately, students tend to have more flexibility regarding hours and dates for an apartment move-in.

What should my roommate and I discuss before we move in together?

How does the roommate selection process work?

Each school is different and it may be a different process from year-to-year, or even building-to-building. Make sure you pay attention to the process and the deadlines. Missing a deadline may cause you to lose housing in an already competitive process.

There are some colleges that have a roommate questionnaire posted online. Be sure to be honest in your answers because this will be a helpful guide for a prospective roommate to know of shared qualities and interests.

What are good questions to ask before you and your roommate move in together?

In today's social-media world, most students know everything about their new roommate in college before they even meet them in person. "This is often the beginning of a failed relationship. You should fight the urge to look up a roommate on social media. Doing so automatically brings up perceived judgments based on what type of music they listen to, what type of books they read, or even what they are doing in their pictures. Instead, students should have a real-life conversation with their roommate, maybe by using FaceTime, Zoom, or any other technology that allows you to speak face-to-face," says Kenrick Ali, California State University, East Bay, director of university union operations. Do not start off your relationship with your roommate by texting, unless it is to quickly say "hi" and set up a face-to-face meeting.

Some schools will provide you with some questions to help you start the conversation. However, here are some good questions that may yield a successful relationship:

Regarding Covid-19, what is their understanding of it, level of concern, and how has it affected their lifestyle?

What are you looking for in a roommate? You should be OK with whatever answer you get as you cannot force anyone to have the type of relationship you want. Also, you never know what will happen as your relationship builds — you may become the best of friends.

What type of schedule do you anticipate? Talk about sleeping, studying, hanging out with friends, and even private, alone time.

What policy do you all want to have about visitors? If you are OK with visitors, is there a time limit? Are you comfortable with visitors sitting on your chair, your bed, etc.?

What are you allowed or not allowed to do in your room? For instance, drinking alcohol, smoking, eating food, sex, etc. Note — be mindful of the policies for your residence hall. Breaking some of those policies could have serious ramifications as severe as eviction or expulsion.

What are you each bringing? Is the other allowed to use it?

Ask some questions that will allow you to get to know your roommate. Ask them about their family; their high-school experience; why they chose the school; what they want to be; what they like doing for fun; their favorite movie; their favorite performer? These types of questions will yield a comfortable dialog between you and your future roommate and will set up the foundation for you to have future conversations, even the difficult ones.

Three tips:

DO NOT let your parents get involved in the conversations. This is YOUR relationship with your roommate, not theirs. "Often parents get too involved and quickly become judgmental about roommates for reasons that are not legitimate. One of the major roles of a parent is to protect their child. Ultimately, this is what they are trying to do for their child when it is the first time they are leaving home. However, some parents often go too far in their involvement and don't understand boundaries with communication and living," says Ali.

Fight the urge to give up on your roommate right away. It is easy to say, "This is not going to work." Many of us live with family members with whom we could have easily made a similar judgment. Part of living with someone new at college is learning about relationships, communication, and compromise. Take advantage of the opportunity you have — it was given for a reason! Also, it is often hard to change rooms as most colleges have used every available space to house as many students as possible. Most schools will have a room-change week to allow you some time to build your relationship before you automatically decide that it won't work. Use this time wisely.

Practice compromise. If you go into the conversation saying "no, no, no," it will never be successful. Remember, you are not the only one paying thousands of dollars to live on campus and to go to that school. Everyone wants to live on campus for an experience. Be respectful of that.

Are there things that you shouldn't bring up before you move in together? What would those things be?

The age-old recommendation has been politics or religion. In this current political climate, it may be helpful to have this conversation with your roommate. An expectation may be that you all don't speak about it in your living space. Colleges and universities exist as a foundation of acceptance and sharing of thoughts, ideas, and people.

"If you are going to college to immediately shut out people with opposing thoughts and views from you, most likely you will not have a great experience," Ali says. "Be comfortable with someone challenging you; be comfortable with learning; be comfortable with understanding someone else's point of view or beliefs; and be comfortable with growth. However, while these are all true, there are certain ideas and behaviors that are not acceptable: discrimination, racism, homophobia, ableism, etc. These do not allow for a welcoming environment and will quickly cause pain for others."

Are there good ways to determine who should bring what to campus? What are those ideas?

First, check out the housing policy regarding what you can have in the room. Some schools will have policies related to the type of refrigerator, or the voltage, or other restrictions. Most schools will provide you with this list in advance, so don't overlook it. Go through that list and eliminate what you cannot bring, and talk to your roommate about the type of things you want in the room to make sure you are both comfortable. Realize, however, you may be sharing a small space, so some things may not fit, or if you have it in the room, it will feel incredibly cramped.

Look at what the school and the housing office provide. For example, if there is a common microwave on your floor or in the building, there is no need to bring one and use the space for it. If you can get the square footage of your room, it may be helpful to map it out with blue tape on the ground, so that you can see how big the space is. Consider that the space will include beds, closets, dressers, desks, and chairs. These all take up space. Build a list with your roommate and determine want you want; whether it will fit in the room; if so, where will it go for easy sharing; and finally, who will bring it.

What are the best ways to handle disagreements between roommates?

Talk about it! Communication is big and is the number-one tool in making sure any relationship is successful. This is a good conversation to have with your roommate. Talk to them about what are things that they could do that would make you angry and make you happy. Talk to them about how you respond to disagreements: Do you get angry, do you yell, do you need some time to yourself?

"In the beginning of your relationship, make sure to spend some time talking about expectations about your roommate relationship. Make sure that one of the expectation topics is communication. Be specific regarding what you need, how you respond, and even consequences for continued disagreements. Don't beat around the bush regarding your expectations — neither one of you — and don't be afraid to ask for what you need, so that you can live comfortably and successfully with them," Ali says. If this fails, most schools have several resources for you to help solve conflict. You can start with your resident assistant or advisor who is typically a student that lives on your floor. They have training to help you and your roommate with conflict. Additionally, available to is your resident director or residence-life coordinator. These are full-time professionals who received training on a variety of topics, including counseling, crisis response, and mediation.

What about picking future roommates?

Get referrals from friends regarding possible roommates for you, and learn more about the people on your hall or in your classes, all of whom could be in your pool of potential future roommates.

What if I have issues with my roommate?

What do you do if you have issues with your roommate?

The best thinking and suggestions would be to stop, think, and analyze what the issues are. Don't react. Stop and think. If I'm the student with the roommate problem, stop and think what's important to me? What do I think matters to the other person? Check in with me — my own self — about my feelings. Figure out what I care about and then think about the approach.

How do I raise it? How do I talk to the other person and when? It's not only what I have to say, but when is a good time?

How do you figure when is the best time to do those things?

"Sometimes it's as simple as checking in with somebody. You could say, 'Hey, there's something on my mind. Is this a good time, and if it's not, could we set up a time to talk?' Be explicit and transparent about it all. If you're the roommate that's upset about something, and I want to talk to my roommate because I'm really upset about the issue, this may not be the best time to talk. Check in with yourself and do a little reflection," says Gail Packer, executive director of the Community Dispute Settlement Center.

For instance, think about what you want to say and how you approach the other person and not barge into that person's space. If it's not a good time for them, they won't be able to listen to you. Both people need to be ready for the conversation. Both you and the other person need to figure when is a good time.

Many colleges have an inventory of a suggested dialog for roommates at the beginning of the school year where they show how to talk through things with a roommate because they are unaccustomed to living with each other. Even though it's a new experience for the roommates, it can be a good roadmap and template to think about how much you know yourself.

For example, it may ask, what's my style? On a scale of 1-10, am I tidy and neat, or loose and messy?

Any tips on how to get along with a roommate, so that you don't get others involved in resolving issues?

The first one is, stop assuming. That's something we do a lot of naturally as human beings. We assume things. We attribute things to people. That can be a problem if you're assuming something about someone that's not accurate. Assuming something that you know is going on with someone — maybe you've seen it before, but it's a different person.

Then the start button is listening and how to be a good, active, engaged listener. That is something that is a bit of a skill these days. We all tend to move quickly and don't take the time to listen to each other.

Pause is to paraphrase and check in with someone to see if you understand what they are saying. You can paraphrase something and say, "Am I getting this right?"

The next one is replay, which is to ask questions. Staying curious is a good mindset to be in when around conflict situations. Ask good questions. Not just questions that you think you know the answers to, but questions that really open a conversation.

Zoom in on interests. Mostly when problems are percolating people fixate on the problem. The person becomes the problem, and even you as the roommate who is upset about something — you could forget what you care about because of the focus on the problem that you're living with in your roommate. Check and see what you really care about and "What do I really need here?" As opposed to, I must have this, or I can't do that, and those are the hardened positions that people get in.

Today, social media is a big deal, and it can really escalate things. So, think before you post. Although she's not sure of its validity, from what Packer has read and heard, "A generation of young people are much more comfortable with the texting and the e-mailing and their interpersonal skills may be a little rough, or they have suffered, or they are undeveloped. In a roommate situation, that's a new deal — you are living with someone you probably don't know, and face-to-face conversation is really going to make a difference."

Are roommate problems typical? How common are roommate issues?

Yes, these problems are common, but not necessarily pervasive. There are problems that roommates can't address and resolve and differences between young people. As Packer says, "Depending upon what those differences are — and when kids go off to college — it's a new world, and they take their family framework with them a little bit or they reject it and leave it totally at home. The values, and behaviors, and habits — they do bring a certain something with them in their suitcase. And when you start to unpack that in a roommate situation, it can be interesting and it could become a problem."

There could be a way to involve someone else that could be a constructive thing. If a student feels stuck and isn't sure how to approach their roommate with something that is bugging them, they could go to the resident advisor. There's some type of student leader in the dorm to have a conversation with and to get some good advice, or comfort coaching. Or, if the person is really upset about something and doesn't feel comfortable about approaching their roommate, the resident advisor can be good at facilitating those conversations. A roommate may not feel they have the skill set and someone like a resident advisor has those talents, and they can help guide the discussion. It doesn't mean it's escalating the discussion.

Resident advisors work in different ways. They can coach the student who is coming to them with a problem and maybe that will help put a few tools in their toolkit, so that the student can do it on their own. If not, the resident advisor could bring the people together and facilitate that conversation.

Where it gets tricky is, sometimes you seek help from a friend. Although sometimes if a friend is loyal to you, they see only your point of view, and they will fire you up even more as opposed to giving you good wisdom or counsel and guidance.

What is the most common issue where roommates disagree?

Packer said she doesn't know the answer to that. However, when she's created scenarios for her training workshops, and she's asked staff at different colleges to give her some typical storylines so she can create conflicts in areas where resident advisors can have some practice, some have mentioned the issue of having guests in the room — whether it's a romantic relationship or too many guests. Other issues include differences in when students need quiet time and when they need lights out, along with unlike sleeping habits. Cultural dimensions can come up as well.

In some ways it might work to normalize the differences. The differences don't necessarily have to be problems or conflicts, Packer says. There are likely to be differences in terms of the approach to being a roommate and the need to be a good roommate, and to recognize that being able to talk things out, to stop and think first, and then to really talk things out can make a difference. Be proactive in that way and don't wait for problems to fester too much because it becomes a huge volcano kept under pressure until it all explodes. "There is a time and place to avoid a situation; a time and place to accommodate someone else; a time and place to assert yourself; a time and place to collaborate; and when to compromise. Those are five different styles of how different people deal with conflict that I often talk about in our training workshops," she said.

"It's based on a framework by Thomas and Kilmann, who were two social scientists that studied human behavior. They identified five different styles of how people respond to conflict: avoid, accommodate, compete, compromise, and collaborate. It's an interesting framework to figure out that there is not one right way to deal with conflict," she added.

These five approaches, or styles, are like tools in the toolbox. What is the right tool for the job? If someone is really upset, maybe you should avoid them for now and get back to talking when each person can be more rational. You can also just give in and accommodate. On the other hand, if you're always accommodating, you don't get your needs met. So, for each one of these styles, there is a time and place as to when to assert and when not to have it always be your way.

You can also take a survey to determine your predominant style. There are influences on us that help us have the style that we do, and everyone has their own influences. The influences are a long list of things, such as gender, family of origin, birth order and sibling lineup, and culture. It's an interesting framework to think about.

What do you do for spending? Do you get a bank card (debit) or a charge card?

What do you do for spending? Do you get a bank card, or a charge card, or both?

When kids go off to college it's usually the first time they have overseen their own personal finances. Typically, there are three types of cards that students will use to pay their bills at college: a prepaid debit card, a credit card, and a debit card.

For a bank card, also known as a debit card, when someone makes a purchase, it takes money out of an account. The account is usually one of two types — checking or savings.

Prepaid debit cards have money loaded on them, and once that money is gone, you can't purchase items. There are no overdrafts, and they are not connected to a bank account. For credit cards, a family can use its existing account and add the student as a user.

What are the best methods to use to pay for things when you are at college?

The positive thing about debit cards is that because the money comes out of an account, if you go over the amount that is in the account, you won't be able to make the purchase. If the debit card is in the parents' name, they will be able to see all items purchased.

The thing going for credit cards is that it may be the best way to protect against fraud among the choice of debit cards, prepaid debit cards, and credit cards.

What's some advice on how to keep track of your spending? Is there a good way to keep track of account numbers and receipts?

A simple way is to put a jar in your drawer and put receipts in there. Then, put a weekly reminder on your phone or in your calendar to record the receipts in the appropriate place. That way you will be sure not to go over your budget limits.

There are other ways, too. You can write down on paper in a notebook what your expenses were after reviewing your receipts. You can also use

Excel, a part of the Microsoft Office suite, to list expenses and account numbers. Keep that on your computer or print it out. You can also find budget apps by doing a Google search using the term "budget app."

Any budget pitfalls to avoid?

- Develop the best money habits that you can.
- Stick to a budget.
- Keep careful records.
- Be responsible with credit cards.
- Have a job either during school or in the summer between school sessions.
- It's OK, and even better, to buy used items.
- Be careful with your money.

Always have some cash and coins available for your use. As an example where this reserve can come in handy, envision a situation when the university's ID card, normally loaded with money to use the washer and dryer in the laundry room, doesn't work and you need coins. Or you need change for the parking meter on campus to avoid a ticket from the university police.

Are there great ways to save some money on purchases while in college? What are those?

Once you're in college, student discounts are available at a lot of places. You should be able to find savings at many businesses in your college town because you are a college student. Anyplace you shop, ask if there's a discount for you.

If you can find coupons, use those, and buy the store brand rather than the brands you've heard of. You're only paying the marketing costs for the brands you're aware of.

Eat in the dining hall because it's already paid for. The dining hall can be a particularly good value if it is all-you-can-eat and you are hungry — especially if you just worked out or were so busy you missed a meal.

Be sure to take advantage of events at college because they are most likely free because of the student activity fee you paid as a part of your tuition. Don't spend to excess when you go out. You don't need to impress your friends to have a good time.

Are there any drawbacks to bank cards and charge cards? What are those?

If you go beyond the limit of what you have in an account with a debit card, you would need to pay extra money, plus interest. Not to mention, some of these cards have fees that occur when there are overdrafts, which means paying money on the interest that accrues.

If a student has a credit card that is part of a parent's account, the person in college might not be inclined to keep spending in check as a parent pays the bill.

What do you do if there's no money left?

On college campuses there are people who can help you to learn more about budgeting. Tell your office of student affairs you would like help to find financial education resources.

What about loaning money to roommates or friends? How can this practice get you into trouble?

Two phrases come to mind that have been frequently repeated by many, "Don't lend money you can't afford to lose. Don't lend money to friends if you want to keep them."

Clubs and Activities

How do you learn more about clubs and activities?

How do you learn more about clubs and activities?

There are numerous ways to do that. Many folks start off with the college's Web site. Every college has a campus-life office. The campus-life office has a listing of college activities. There could be several hundred or thousands of activities — it depends on what college you attend. Colleges also use Web-based software where individual clubs use the program to build a micro site using Web pages. These groups then post their calendar of activities or their officers. This information usually appears on a campus activities site for the university.

For incoming students, the orientation and admissions offices will also have campus activities information, or they might have a social-media channel or a Facebook group. Once the student gets to campus, typically at the beginning of the academic year, there are activities fairs or campus organization exhibitions. Oftentimes, groups on campus host an activity on a certain day during the welcome week or during an orientation program. Once again, that could be 100 or 1,000 student organizations giving out information to students about what they do.

A university Web site, online, social media, and the activities office are the best ways to learn about what is available for students.

Are the campus newspaper or the campus radio station good sources to find information?

If the college has these, that could be a good way. But a full listing might not necessarily appear in a campus newspaper. However, an organization may advertise events that are happening throughout the year in that publication. If a group has the resources and know-how to advertise on a campus-run TV or radio station, that might be a way to get information.

Are there any clubs to join if you are a freshman?

It depends on your interests. That would be the first place to start. What are your hobbies, interests, passions, and coursework? Then, think about what is out there for you. There are some organizations that maybe

COLLEGE, COVID, AND QUESTIONS

you can't join as a first-year student. In the event you could, if you're living on campus, the residence hall has an association and the student government encourages people to join. Both of those groups are an easy way to get involved right off the bat. As for student government itself, there may be a programming board that students might gravitate toward because those are the more visible — and some of the first things — a first-year student might see.

How about if you are a sophomore, or an upperclassman — a junior or senior? Can you think of some things that may be more interesting to those upperclassmen?

The Honor societies, based on your career interests and coursework, could be interesting. "You can take a leadership role in those organizations and it's advised to do so when possible," Jameson Root, National Association for Campus Activities, says. "There are so many things students can do. For example, if you are interested in the newspaper, you can be a member of the editorial board or a staff writer. Students can participate or run an organization or be on a governing board."

Are there clubs that have a certain grade-point average to join or you must be a certain grade level to participate?

Most of the fraternity and sorority organizations have a grade-point average you must maintain. There are honorary societies, such as Mortarboard. It depends on the campus and organization. Sometimes, if you are with the student government or an athlete, you need to have a certain grade-point average. Often, when you talk about the leadership roles within an organization, such as president or secretary, that's often where the grade-point average comes into play. It's not hard to imagine if you're a person studying accounting and you want to be the president of the chess club that you need a certain grade-point average.

What are some advantages to students who join clubs and activities?

"There's a lot of research noting academic performance is higher and retention rates are better for those who participate in clubs and activities. Some benefits to joiners include closeness, connections, and having friend groups," Root says. If you're a first-year student new to college and become a member of an organization that has upperclassmen, you're getting to meet those folks and build friendships, but you also gain potential mentors who can help you through your 101 courses that everyone must take instead of navigating those by yourself. You can imagine during times of crisis, like we're having now with the coronavirus, you have a support group and a network to fall back on. That's helpful. Or, to move out of your dorm, you have friends to help you and chip in.

Depending on the type of organization — and some are mission-based — let's say you're in a volunteer group and you're building houses for Habitat for Humanity. Yes, you're benefiting yourself, but you're also helping your community and society. It's important for students to have a chance to participate in organizations like this.

There might also be scholarship opportunities through certain groups. A nonmember might not have access to those chances. National programs and leadership conferences offer a lot outside the college and can open possibilities. Oftentimes, from these clubs and activities, you can network and find a job as well. There might be alumni from a club who come back to visit, and you actively make connections with them. It often happens in the fraternity and sorority community. It can happen in the athletic community; it can happen in honor societies and volunteer groups. Students make strong connections because of being a part of that group.

Are there any disadvantages if you participate in a club or activity?

"The disadvantages only exist when folks go too far," says Root. "They want to go join everything and think they can do that. There are only so many hours in a day and academic coursework." He says, in college, there's a balance between what you want to get involved in, but also how you want to perform academically. "Having a bit of a plan when you go in is important. You can think, I want to get involved in these things and try these out, but be OK with saying after a couple of weeks or months, let's step away from an activity to focus on academics, and I can always come back."

Is there any advice on learning more about clubs and activities?

Covid-19 has put restrictions on many group activities, including the number of participants for both on and off-campus events. There can be severe penalties for violations, including suspension or expulsion from school. Look for activities impacted the least. As for using student recreation centers, consider individual workouts when using weight equipment.

It is important to do research. Look at things and do events you haven't tried before. You can imagine going to a big university with 1,500 different student organizations, which can be overwhelming. Take the time before coming to the university, or during college breaks, to examine things. There are constantly new clubs and activities popping up. Reevaluate and think about what you're trying to accomplish. Are there groups out there that can help you do that?

Often overlooked are the professional staff who work on the college and university campuses. They are there to help students navigate the process, so visiting the campus activities office or the community service office is helpful. For those staff, their job is to help students get engaged. If they ask school personnel, they may learn about clubs they weren't aware of. Something for the students to know is that university staff like when students visit. That's why the personnel are there: to engage and help. Those are fun conversations to have, and staff can learn who the students are and discover how to help them during their time at the university.

The Dean's Office is a central office, and most schools have one. They will send you to the right office, if you don't know who to ask a question.

What should a student look for in a club or activity?

Look for something that interests you. Every club or organization exists for some purpose. Examine that purpose and see how it aligns with you. What are you studying and what do you want to do in your career? What are the organizations that directly relate to that? For example, there's a business honor society, and you want to study business. Do you join that organization? Tangentially, you say, "OK, I'm studying business, and I'm really interested in the marketing and communications aspects. Do I want to join the newspaper where I can oversee communications, or be the secretary who does skills and practices them through an organization?"

That's a thing to think through. What do you want to do and how can you accomplish that through those positions? It can be as simple as you really like to play football, so you're going to join the rec football league. Or, you want to be a doctor, so you're going to be in a certain medical group.

What tips do you have when a student joins a club or activity, so a student can get the most out of it?

Attend the meetings and events. Some organizations have weekly or biweekly meetings and gatherings. Know when those are and when they happen, and try to go to them, if possible. Build relationships with people in the organization. Instead of being just a member, as you get more comfortable with the organization through the years and as you move up in college, take a role that gives you a chance to do more in life. A student organization is almost a laboratory or an environment to practice what you may not learn in the classroom, and it offers skills essential for the workforce. You may learn about communication, conflict management, and leadership. By participating in a club or helping with an event, a student can learn how to manage their peers.

Most colleges work hard to help, and they realize students are learning life skills through clubs. Additionally, university staff try to offer conferences and events where students can learn those leadership roles and skills. Campus life, student life, and campus activities offices are a good clearinghouse to gather information about those conferences, and many groups often maintain calendars about events that are happening. Some universities will have a leadership office coordinate a conference. A conference will usually happen every semester or every quarter in a regular pattern. Workshops may also occur at different times.

Therefore, it is challenging for students because there are so many ways to get information, and colleges do it differently. But, at least there's one place to start — either the Dean's Office or the student-life office. From there, you can connect to more specific things that are of interest to you.

For major events happening, the student newspaper is good because it usually advertises those things.

There is so much out there. Although it may be hard to navigate, there are so many benefits that come out of belonging to a club or activity.

How do intramurals work on campus?

What are some benefits to participating in intramurals?

It's important to find ways to continue to stay active and to take breaks from the rigors of school. However, team sports and intramural sports may be limited by Covid-19.

Some of the traditional benefits of participating in intramurals have been physical exercise and a way to blow off steam and the pressures of college. But on a deeper level, intramural participation helps students form a connection to campus and shape their social networks. These things enhance a student's sense of belonging, and can help with retention to graduation. Students often make lifelong friends and memories while playing intramurals.

Intramurals are a great way to meet students, make more friends, and get good exercise. Exercise is good for the brain and a great way to get your mind off homework, plus it reduces stress. It's an excellent way to stay healthy, says a Radford student.

Think of it as camaraderie, competition, exercise, and fun — all in one place.

What are the drawbacks to participating in intramurals?

For some, there is a financial barrier to participating in intramurals. Across the country, most programs charge some sort of fee to play. There are some schools that can offer these services for free, but the vast majority charge. Another drawback can be the competitive environment. Some students are just looking to have fun, while others want to compete in a sport they love. When these goals clash, it can create an experience that is not fun for one or both teams. With competition also comes conflict. That is also a drawback — sometimes competition gets the best of people, and the game ends with conflict instead of fun.

If you don't have good time-management skills, intramurals can take away time from your studies. It could be risky and tempting to decide to play a game rather than study for a big test the next day, says a Radford student. Many times, leagues do have scheduled game times and a requirement that a student attend, which might be hard at the end of a semester when many are studying for tests or completing projects.

What's the typical process when signing up for intramurals?

Most schools now run online registration through Web sites such as IMLeagues. Participants can register with a team or as a free agent. Most schools list the sport, league (men's, women's, or coed), division (competitive or recreational), and the time of play. Students can then select what and when they want to play. Sports feature a variety of formats, from weekly games during a season followed by playoffs, to one-day tournaments and special events.

Intramurals are different times of the year. You can sign up or request to play on a specific team. You can also create a team based on your dorm, your major, or a Living Learning Community. For instance, a Living Learning Community with people who want to go into the teaching profession might form a squad, a Radford student says.

How about if you're new to campus and want to participate on a team? How do you find teammates?

Students find teams in many ways. They use classmates and floormates. They use members of other clubs and organizations they are a part of. They compete with other coworkers who hold student jobs. They can also sign up as free agents. In that case, teams that need more players can contact the free agent and add the person to their team. The intramurals office will also reach out to all free agents and try to organize them into teams, too.

If you don't know anyone the best way may be to go to the gym where they have shootarounds, for example for basketball. You could meet people on the court. It's fine to ask for placement on a team with random people because that's a way to expand your circle of friends, so consider that as an option, a Radford student says. Many people enjoy joining others regardless of their major or dormitory — they want to be part of a group.

How about if you're doing something like a sport where you compete as an individual, take for instance Ping-Pong or bowling. Are there opportunities to participate in intramurals for those types of things?

Intramurals come in all formats and varieties. Some schools run individual and dual sports, just like team sports. "We run things like singles and doubles tennis, badminton, racquetball, pickleball, and table tennis. We offer over 40 different activities and sports throughout the year for students to choose from," says Ashley Lax, University of Wisconsin-Madison's assistant director of sports programs.

Are there typically teams made up of people who live in a dorm or who have the same major?

Many teams consist of floormates, or a group of House Fellows. There are also teams formed from registered student organizations. So, there may be an engineering club on campus and that club may sign up as a team to play intramurals. You also have teams consisting of students in the same major, dorm, student group, or fraternity and sorority. Intramurals often build camaraderie among their group.

Any advice for someone who's looking to participate in intramurals?

Overall, students just need to be willing to try something new and put themselves out there a bit. They are typically going to find like-minded people who share common interests that they can connect with on campus. And they never know where those connections may lead.

Get out there and sign up. Regardless if you know anyone or not, it's a great way to meet a diverse group of people while also having a good time. You don't need to be in a league. You can go to the recreation center and sign up, and there you'll meet people who have interest in a similar sport — a laid-back and relaxed way to meet new people, says a Radford student.

Look for signs at the rec center and dorms announcing the formation of intramural teams, a Radford student says.

How do club sports work on campus?

How do club sports work in college?

It depends on the college because it varies from campus to campus based on student involvement. The general concept is that these are student organizations primarily being sport- related and completely student-run with advisors or professional staff dedicated to their education and development.

"Many people would compare club-sport programs to being the "junior varsity" sports of college athletics. The big difference is most student organizations that are club sports have club-sport officers, leaders, or an executive board who are students and lead the club. This provides them with significant experiential learning experiences on how to lead their peers; manage time; self-manage; plan travel, in some cases; event planning; and budgeting," says Hannah Roberts, a sport and youth program specialist at East Carolina University. Students are basically running a small business. Some club sports are competitive, and some may just be instructional or recreational in nature to teach their sport or activity.

Do you need to pay to play club sports?

It depends again on the institution and the club. Many club sports have membership dues just to cover the minimum expenses to travel, compete, and host events. Each club may have different criteria for what the dues may cover, but that is based on the student organization and leadership of the club at that time, which gives them the opportunity to budget and make those important decision-making skills.

What sports are typically offered at the club level?

It depends, but commonly you will see a lot of the Olympic-style sports: swimming, soccer, basketball, and volleyball. It depends on program capability to accept certain clubs due to budget, facilities, or general student interest in starting a specific club sport. "At East Carolina University, there are all kinds of sports: baseball; bass fishing; boxing; cheerleading; cross country and track; dance (hip hop/jazz); disc golf; equestrian; fencing; field hockey; figure skating; golf; ice hockey; men's and women's lacrosse; martial arts; weightlifting (Olympic style); Raas Indian dance; climbing; men's and women's rugby; ski-snowboard; men's and women's soccer; softball; swimming; tennis; men's and women's ultimate frisbee; men's and women's volleyball; wrestling; and yoga," says Roberts.

What are the differences between club and intramural sports in college?

Many ask this common question of campus staff, but intramurals are more of an opportunity to meet new people while also being able to play sports and activities competitively or just for fun. Some club sports have this similar, if not the same philosophy, but more times than not there is a more competitive nature to club sports. These are organized club-sport teams that travel and/or host events that represent the university locally, regionally, and nationally. Most club sports have conferences, leagues, or governing bodies that set standards for competition. Club sports also have a unique educational approach with club sport officers directing them with intentional meetings and presentations.

Are there tryouts for club sports?

It depends on the club and institution. Some colleges do not allow club sports to have tryouts, but some do allow tryouts. This can also depend on the function and the ability of the organization to support club members.

Travel

How do you get home? Are there apps people can use?

What are some ways that students can find ways to get home for a weekend or school break?

There are many ways to get home. If you need to take a plane, you can use frequent-flier miles or points from credit cards to qualify for a no-cost flight. But there are also Web sites available to students that offer discounts. For instance, American Airlines offers a student discount for some flights from a list of universities.

If you live closer to campus, you might consider a bus like Greyhound, Megabus, or BoltBus, which Greyhound owns. Both BoltBus and Megabus have Wi-Fi at no cost, a power outlet for each rider to plug in electronics, and comfortable seats. Currently, BoltBus travels to cities on the East Coast and in the Northeast, as well as parts of the West Coast. You can buy tickets over the phone or online and confirm a seat with a reservation. Megabus goes to more than 100 cities and university campuses, and you can reserve seats by using a smartphone or computer.

Traveling to 2,400 North American destinations, Greyhound also offers Wi-Fi, power outlets, and expanded legroom. Additionally, you can take Greyhound to make connections to places not served by rail-service-provider Amtrak. To purchase a ticket, call on the phone; visit places such as convenience stores and gas stations; go online; head to a Greyhound bus station; or use the phone app. Greyhound does not assign seats.

Amtrak trains travel to 46 states and 500 places over 21,400 miles of track. To book travel, go online, use the mobile app, phone, purchase at the station, or go through a travel agent. Some of Amtrak's amenities on routes may include a food car, power outlets, tray table, and reclining seats.

Ask each of these companies if they offer student travel discounts to get the best possible price for travel. Use a search engine and type in "student discounts" to locate cheaper fares for plane, bus, train, and car travel.

If planes, trains, and buses are not for you, try carpooling with a friend who has a home near yours. You can ask around your dorm or apartment building, post on the college Facebook page, use Craigslist, or list your need on a message board on campus. Be ready to split gas costs with whomever totes you home.

Zipcar is available at some universities for students to sign up for a car by the hour or by the day. The company pays expenses for gas, insurance, registration, and maintenance. Students must be at least 18 with a valid driver's license at a university that offers Zipcar, or 21 with a valid license. To register for a car, sign up with the service.

Enterprise CarShare also has programs through different universities and is temporarily suspending its program at some universities in September 2020 because of the coronavirus. However, you can rent at nearby Enterprise Rent-A-Car locations. The value of Enterprise CarShare is the ability to find a car close to your college campus available by the hour or for one or more days. The cars are ready anytime and parked in specific spaces.

For students between the ages of 18 and 20, or where law requires it, you can become a member. Same for those at age 21. Not sure if your campus participates? Head to the Enterprise CarShare program locations page and see if your school appears. There, you'll find more information about how to become a member and the costs.

Are there any apps people can use? Which of those are best?

To find a ride home, try Wheeli, where you can ask college students from your school and others for transportation. Use your college e-mail address to register with Wheeli. Search for a ride from other drivers. Once you select a ride, a seat price for passengers is determined based on costs for tolls and gas. Pay through the site with no cash exchanged, and enjoy your trip home. This free app allows you to participate as a rider or driver.

Try SpotHero to reserve parking at a lot or garage, sometimes at a reduced cost. This app allows you to set aside a space by using your phone to investigate prices and options.

Waze is a terrific resource to get you through traffic nightmares. It provides directions, road alerts, and live traffic maps to your destination. This phone app can even help you circumvent tolls by getting where you want to go via back roads. Plus, it tells you when you'll arrive at the place you want to go. Available as a phone app.

The phone app GasBuddy looks at where you are to nail the least expensive gas price, allowing you to save money. Users update the gas prices to make sure you have the latest information. The app features 27 ways to save bucks at 150,00 gas stations in the United States.

TripIt gathers your airline, car rental, and hotel e-mail confirmations to make an itinerary for your trip. A free app, you review trip details on a phone or computer. It also allows you to store travel documents in one place.

Want to make a list of what to pack for where you're heading? Get PackPoint, another free app that also helps you save money by packing the right things and not spending extra cash on checked baggage that exceeds airline weight limits.

Worry no more about vehicle breakdowns with Urgent.ly. Available 24/7, this app helps with towing, jump-starts, tire changes, delivering gas, and car lockouts. Best yet, there are no dues to belong. Use this service in the U.S. and Puerto Rico.

Use Wanderu to examine bus, train, and airline options when traveling in the U.S. and Europe. You can find your travel location, check pricing, and reserve tickets using the free app or by going online. A great feature is the ability to look at different ways to get home for the best price.

What tips do you have when trying to find a ride home?

Connect with a student with a car driving to your general area. The school may have specific apps just for this purpose.   Help share in paying for the gas, tolls, and other incidentals. There may be fewer opportunities to do this until Covid-19 passes.

If you lack a method to find rides, try your school's office of residence life or office of student affairs for suggestions.

How about if you live across the country or overseas? What do you do? Can you stay in the dorm over break? What options are open to you?

For traveling to other parts of the country or internationally, there may be Covid-19 restrictions, including a required quarantine for a set number of days and even outright prohibitions on entering certain countries.

Not every college has the same policy, but for students unable to leave for break, such as Thanksgiving, winter, or spring vacation, you may be able to stay in your dorm room at an extra cost. While many dining halls and campus restaurants may have reduced hours, others may close for the duration of break.

Many campuses have an office that helps international students or those who live far from campus. See if office personnel can offer guidance on staying with a professor's family or another family in town. You might even fill a role for a local family in doing something like house sitting while the family is away. Don't forget to ask if any of your friends or acquaintances can have you as a house guest, too.

If you can't leave at the end of the school term, perhaps you can go to summer school and live in a dorm.

In any case, if the issue of living far away is important, ask colleges about their policy of living in the dorms during breaks. Their answer will help you decide whether the school is right for you and meets your needs.

What about if you have a disability? Are there transit options available? Are there special apps available — say you use a wheelchair and you need to get home. Can you use a plane, train, bus?

With the Americans with Disabilities Act, wheelchair users now have access to buses, trains, and planes. Check with each of these modes of transit to learn their policies.

Do most universities provide transportation to nearby large cities? For instance, Virginia Tech provides a shuttle for students heading to northern Virginia.

BreakShuttle bills itself as "the largest provider of college break transportation services in the United States." Now, it services universities in the New England, South, Midwest, and Mid-Atlantic regions, as well as Texas. A part of Wells + Associates since 2017, BreakShuttle's Web site notes it provides "direct, reliable, safe, and affordable transportation during academic breaks. With BreakShuttle, universities make their campuses more accessible and help families reduce the financial and logistical stress of having a child in college.

"BreakShuttle's full-time staff works with universities to coordinate travel arrangements for students. The service is fully insured with comfortable vehicles operated by responsible, courteous drivers."

What things should a student do to prepare for the trip home?

If you have items that are no longer necessary for your dorm or apartment, bring those home. This includes clothes or things that you never use that take up space. If you need to study over break, bring your laptop, binders with class notes, textbooks, graphing calculator (if necessary), and cell phone, plus your student ID. Don't forget your laptop charger. If it's winter at home, bring your coat and boots, if you anticipate snow, plus a hat and gloves.

You can do laundry at home and that lessens what you need to pack. If there are any school supplies you might need, sometimes they are cheaper at home. Before you leave your home to return to school, be sure to pack everything you brought with you.

Any advice as to the timing as to when to begin your search for a ride home?

It's never too early to look for a ride home, whether it be by bus, train, plane, or car. Pre-purchase your ticket in advance so you get a seat, and if there is a student discount, make sure it is applied. Don't forget to bring your student ID with you to get the price reduction.

Because most college students go home at similar times for Thanksgiving, winter, and spring breaks, there can be competition to get a seat. Stay on top of the school break schedule to ensure you are not the straggler on campus because you didn't make plans in time.

What things should you bring home?

All your dirty laundry.

INDEX

About the Author

Suzy Beamer Bohnert is the author of many acclaimed books for readers. Her award-winners include *Game-Day Youth: Learning Baseball's Lingo,* a Mom's Choice Award-winner for "Most Outstanding Nonfiction Children's Book"; *Game-Day Youth: Learning Basketball's Lingo,* named Best Books for Teen Boys by the New Hampshire Library Media Association; *Game-Day Youth: Learning Football's Lingo,* an Honorable Mention Award for nonfiction in the Readers' Favorite International Book Awards; and the *Game-Day Goddess Sports Series, 3-Volume Set,* selected as Best Books for College Students by StudentAdvisor.com, a Washington Post Co. *Game-Day Goddess: Learning Baseball's Lingo, Game-Day Youth: Learning Basketball's Lingo, Game-Day Youth: Learning Baseball's Lingo* and *Game-Day Youth: Learning Football's Lingo* each won the Readers' Favorite Five-Star Award.

The recipient of nineteen national awards for writing excellence, she lives in northern Virginia with her husband and family.

**Review Suzy Beamer Bohnert's books
on www.amazon.com and www.bn.com**